what you
didn't know
about

GOD'S THRONE

let it out of your box

DARRELL MCMANUS

I0149080

What You Didn't Know About God's Throne
Copyright © 2015 by Darrell McManus

Unless otherwise noted, all scripture quotations in this volume are taken from the Holy Bible: New King James Version®. Copyright © 1982 by Thomas Nelson, Inc. Used by permission. All rights reserved.

Scripture quotations taken from the New American Standard Bible®, Copyright © 1960, 1962, 1963, 1968, 1971, 1972, 1973, 1975, 1977, 1995 by The Lockman Foundation Used by permission. (www.Lockman.org)

Scripture quotations taken from the Amplified® Bible, Copyright © 1954, 1958, 1962, 1964, 1965, 1987 by The Lockman Foundation Used by permission. (www.Lockman.org)

Scripture quotations taken from the King James Version of the Bible. (Public Domain)

Scripture quotations taken from the Darby Version of the Bible. (Public Domain)

RevMedia Publishing
P.O. Box 5172
Kingwood, TX 77325
www.revmediapublishing.com

ISBN: 978-1-7345273-3-9
Printed in the United States of America

Purchase additional copies of this book and more titles from Darrell McManus at your favorite online and local retailers. www.darrellmcmanus.com

DEDICATION

I dedicate this book and give all praise to the Father, the Son, and the Holy Spirit for entrusting me with this revelation. God, you are truly awesome!

I dedicate this book to my beautiful wife, Cindy, who is my lover, my friend, the mother of our children and my faithful partner in the ministry. I love yo. Without your spiritual and emotional support, this book would not have been possible. I love you, Babe! You are the best!

Finally, I dedicate this book to Pastors Ross and Beverly Cunningham and congregation of The Master's Gateway Church in Milano, Texas. Thank you for providing me the platform during "The Move Of God Services" to minister on God's Throne. The thirteen messages I delivered on God's Throne are the primary source for this book, and I am eternally grateful.

ACKNOWLEDGMENTS

I would like to gratefully acknowledge the following Biblical translations used in the writing of this book:

The King James Version (KJV)

The New King James Version (NKJV)

The New American Standard Bible (NASB)

The Amplified Bible (AMP)

Darby Translation (Darby)

CONTENTS

CHAPTER 1

INTRODUCTION TO GOD'S THRONE

The First Vision: God Riding a Cherub

I was blessed to have had two amazing visions about God the Father. The first vision occurred one day, as I was driving the church van, heading north on U.S. Hwy 77 between Hallettsville and Schulenburg, Texas. My wife, Cindy, was in the passenger seat, and my youngest son, Joshua, was asleep on one of the seats in the back of the van. We were traveling about 70 mph, on our way to minister at an Awakening Meeting in The Woodlands, Texas, when, all of a sudden, I had a vision. I saw God the Father, in the sky in front of me, riding a cherub. The whole vision took place within the space of a few seconds. God was kicked back, as if He held the reigns to this angelic being, and He burst out laughing, as if to say, "I've got this!" I heard Him say to me, "I mount the cherub."

The vision was so real that I took my hands off the steering wheel and was in the process of undoing my seatbelt when Cindy, with great emotion, said to me, "What are you doing?" She grabbed the steering wheel, a concerned look on her face.

I said, "I've got to find the scripture, 'I mount the cherub.' It's got to be in the Bible. He just quoted it to me!" My wife said, "Keep your hands on the wheel; I'll find it." Cindy found two scriptures that spoke of God riding a cherub: 2 Samuel 22:11 and Psalm 18:10.

I found a place to pull off the road in Schulenburg. I told Cindy, "I saw the Father. He was riding a cherub!" I began to weep.She drove the rest of the way to the meeting, as I sat beside her and wept.

What a powerful meeting we had that night! I didn't know it then, but the Lord told me later, "I came down for you." God literally came down on a cherub to rescue us out of one of the greatest trials we'd ever faced!

The Second Vision: God's Throne Descending

The second vision occurred during a time of intense worship, as I was caught up in the realm of the Spirit. I saw God's throne moving between Heaven and Earth. I could tell that it had more than one level. The throne was awesome! Seeing that huge entourage coming down has forever changed my life!

In this book, we will take a look at God's Throne: where it is, what it is, and why it is important to us. Psalm 103:19 (AMP) tells us, "*The Lord has established His throne in the heavens.*" If your Bible translation reads "heaven," then you should substitute the word "heavens," because the Hebrew word *shamayim* is always plural. It is a masculine plural noun meaning "heavens, the abode of God, or the universe."

How many heavens are there? The answer is *three.* I want to establish this, because it is foundational for where we're going in this study. God established His throne in the heavens.

For years, I had the idea that God's throne was in a room. I will submit to you, according to my study in the Word, it is not. The throne is simply too big to be housed in a room. When we get into this study, we will discover that God's throne is so big, in fact, that He gave just a partial view of it to three different men of God: it is so big that no man could take it all in from the earthly view!

God gave Ezekiel the view from beneath. He gave Isaiah the view from above. And He gave John the panoramic, eye level view. After all, heaven is not a plane—it's not flat, like a sheet of paper. Heaven is 1,500 miles in every direction: its length, breadth and height are the same. In Isaiah 6, you'll find the seraphim were standing above it.

Now, let's go a little bit further. Let's look at this verse again: *"The Lord has established His throne in the heavens, and His kingdom..."* God is putting two things together here. He's established His throne in the heavens, and His kingdom. So God is equating His throne with the kingdom. He established His throne in the heavens, and His kingdom rules over all.

In other words, where the throne is, the highest level of authority in the kingdom resides. And if we can access the throne, we can access that which will rule over any sickness, over any problem. I don't care what you're dealing with. If you can access the throne, and get the throne to come to your house, the problem will be obliterated. Why? Because God has established His throne in the heavens, and His kingdom rules over all.

The scripture goes on, *"Bless the Lord, you His angels, who excel in strength, who do His word, heeding, [or harkening] the voice of His word."* When we put God's word into our mouths, it releases the angels. *"Bless the Lord, all you His hosts, you ministers of His, who do His pleasure. Bless the Lord, all His works, in all places of His dominion. Bless the Lord, o my soul."*

Now let's look at Isaiah. I'm going to show you some other scriptures that clearly indicate that God is not locked into a "throne room." I hear many preachers talk about this "throne room." I'm going to give you some scriptures that may jog your thinking about the throne and where it truly resides.

God started revealing His throne to me when we were hidden out in the country, and it changed my life forever. I've not heard it preached anywhere. I got it straight from Him. It's a religious idea that God the Father has just been sitting up there on the throne for thousands of years. And that's because we haven't had enough Word on the subject.

Look at Isaiah 66:1 (Darby) with me: "[*Thus says the Lord:]* *'The heavens are My throne.*" That doesn't say that His throne is *in* heaven; it says, "*The heavens are My throne, and the earth is My footstool.*" That's not a room.

Let's finish. He says, "*Where is the house that you will build Me?*" In other words, "A house can't contain Me; certainly, a room can't." It is not a "throne room." God is saying, "Where is the house that you're going to build that can contain Me? The whole heavens are My throne. The earth is My footstool. "*Where is the place of My rest? For all those things My hand has made. And all those things exist,' says the Lord.*"

Now turn to Psalm 104, beginning with verse 1. "*O, Lord my God, You are very great. You are clothed with honor and majesty, who cover Yourself with light.*" You know that song, *How Great is our God*, where it says, "He wraps himself in light." Psalm 104:1 is where that verse comes from. He is a great God! Don't relegate Him to some little room; that is a religious idea. If I polled Christians across the world, 90-some percent would proclaim that there is a "throne room," because that's how little of the Word we've had on this. My hope is that as we study this topic, you're going to have the religious scales removed from your eyes, concerning who God is. Your faith is going to expand. You'll say, "Why have I been so limited in what I believe for?"

Back to Psalm 104: "*Who cover Yourself with light as with a garment. Who stretch out the heavens like a curtain.*" All of the heavens—the first, second, and third heaven—He stretches out like a curtain. That boggles our minds. And God should boggle our minds. "*He lays the beams of His upper chambers in the waters. Who makes the clouds His chariot.*" He's riding today. We're going to find out in this book where He goes. He's looking for something. And we're going to be the people that He's seeking. The Bible says, "*The eyes of the Lord are roaming throughout the whole earth.*" You don't have eyes unless you want to see something. Smith Wigglesworth said God will pass over a million homes to get to yours, if you'll just show Him some faith. Jesus even said, "*Will the Son of Man find faith when I come back?*" Will He find faith? According to scripture, He will, in us. If it's in His Word, we can believe it, even if we don't understand it.

Let's go a little bit further: "*Who walks on the wings of the wind. Who makes His angels spirits, His ministers a flame of fire.*" If God is present, there'll be fire. He doesn't *have* fire—He *is* a consuming fire.

Now let's look at Psalm 45:6. It will help to lay a foundation for this teaching. "*Your throne, O God, is forever and ever; a scepter of righteousness is the scepter of Your kingdom.*" And Psalm 103:19 (AMP) says, "*The Lord has established His throne in the heavens, and His kingdom rules over all.*" Here's the throne and the kingdom put together again. In other words, in order for us to have kingdom authority, we're going to have to have throne level authority and power.

I looked up the Hebrew word for *scepter*. It is *shevet*, which means, "rod, scepter, an instrument with the mark of authority, a symbol of rulership." In other words, wherever God's throne is, His kingdom authority resides; and wherever His kingdom is operating, the kingdom will rule. And what is the kingdom of God? It is righteousness, peace, and joy in the Holy Ghost.

Where is the highest level of authority in any kingdom? The throne. What did Pharaoh tell Joseph? In Genesis 41:38-40, he said, *"You shall be over my house, and all my people shall be ruled according to your word; only in regard to the throne will I be greater than you."* In other words, the throne is the highest level of authority in a kingdom.

Since we're establishing a foundation for this teaching, let's go to the Old Testament book of Daniel. Daniel 7:9-10 describes the Great White Throne Judgment mentioned in the book of Revelation. This is a more in-depth view of what's going to happen. Verse 9 says, *"I watched till thrones were put in place, and the Ancient of Days was seated."* Some translations say "cast down; some say, "put or set in place."

In other words, the Ancient of Day's throne was not there originally: it *moved* to this place. *"The Ancient of Days was seated; His garment was white as snow, and the hair of His head was like pure wool. His throne was a fiery flame, its wheels..."* Wheels? Yes, God the Father's throne has wheels, and it's always had wheels. His throne was fire, and the wheels on it were wheels of fire. A wagon doesn't need wheels, unless it moves. Your car doesn't need wheels, unless it moves. Little toy trucks don't need wheels, unless they move. And certainly, God's throne doesn't need wheels, unless it moves.

God put that in the Scripture because He wanted it to be revealed, so that we could understand more of how He operates. The more we can understand how God operates, the more we're going to understand His ways. The more you understand His ways, the more you'll know how to get Him to show up in a meeting; how to get Him to fall with glory in a meeting. He wants us to know.

"His throne was a fiery flame, its wheels a burning fire; a fiery stream issued and came forth from before Him. A thousand thousands ministered to Him; ten thousand times ten thousand stood before Him. The court was seated, and the books were opened."

This is a picture of the Great White Throne Judgment. The reason why the throne will have to move out of the third heaven for this judgment is that sin will never enter the third heaven. That's why the thrones were cast down. They were set in place. God chose a place where He could deal with sinners, and not violate the holiness of the third heaven. Again, whether that word is translated as "cast down," or whether it's translated as "set in place," the Hebrew word is the same: *remah*. There's no way to translate the word "remah" that would indicate that the throne was already there. And the verse says, "thrones," which leads to the conclusion that they all were able to move.

Now, let's jump over to the New Testament book of Revelation, chapter 4, verses 1-2: *"After these things, I looked, and behold, a door standing open in heaven. And the first voice which I heard was like a trumpet, speaking with me, saying, 'Come up here, and I will show you things which must take place after this.' Immediately, I was in the Spirit; and behold, a throne set in heaven and One sat on the throne."*

The original Greek word translated "set" or "stood" or "sitting" is *keimai*. It means, "put or set in place, or laid down." John was caught up into the third heaven, and a throne was laid down or put or set in place. This Greek word is almost an identical translation to the Hebrew counterpart we discussed in Daniel 7. He was caught up in heaven, and the throne was set or put in place. *"And there was One who sat on the throne."* Who was that? None other than the Father. The Father wants to reveal who He is, to those who want to know.

Now go with me to Hebrews 12, starting with verse 22: *"But you have come to Mount Zion and to the city of the living God, the heavenly Jerusalem, to an innumerable company of angels, to the general assembly and church of the firstborn, who are registered in heaven."* Jesus was the firstborn among many brethren. And we are also in there somewhere. Those who are registered in heaven, God says you are registered to this church: the church of the firstborn.

"You have come to . . . God, the Judge of all, to the spirits of just men made perfect, to Jesus the Mediator of the new covenant, and to the blood of sprinkling that speaks better things than that of Abel. See to it that you do not refuse Him who speaks. For if they did not escape who refused Him who spoke on earth, how much more shall we not escape if we turn away from Him who speaks from heaven, whose voice then shook the earth; but now He has promised, saying, 'Yet once more I l shake not only the earth, but also heaven.' Now this, 'Yet once more,' indicates the removal of those things that are being shaken, as of things

that are made, that the things which cannot be shaken may remain. Therefore, since we are receiving a kingdom which cannot be shaken, let us have grace, by which we may serve God acceptably with reverence and godly fear. For our God is a consuming fire."

Today we're living in a time, in this country, where everything is being shaken. But I want to encourage you, if you operate in the kingdom, you won't be shaken. The kingdom cannot be shaken. The throne cannot be shaken. The scepter cannot be shaken. God established His throne in the heavens. And His kingdom rules over all. That's why it can't be shaken, because it rules. When someone comes against us, the kingdom will rule.

That's as far as we'll go in this chapter. We've established some things here:

The throne can, and does, move; that kingdom level authority is synonymous with God's throne; and that God established His throne in the heavens, and His kingdom rules over all.

CHAPTER 2

Ezekiel's Vision of God's Throne

Just to review, we looked at some of these Scriptures in the previous chapter. God says that He's established His throne in the *shamayim*, the heavens, which means the throne can move throughout the three heavens. It'll move from the third to the second to the first. What is the first heaven? The atmosphere; this air we breathe. What is the second heaven? The cosmos: the place of the stars. What is the third heaven? The sides of the north. That's not the North Pole; it is due north. There's a place in outer space called due north. Science can't get a handle on it, and they won't get a handle on it, because it's another dimension, the realm in which God dwells. And that's what Ezekiel saw. We're going to take a closer look at what this prophet of God saw in this chapter.

In our minds, we've had this limited view of God, dwelling in a room called *the Throne Room*. I want you to shed that limited view. And the Scriptures are going to help you do it. Don't take it from me, unless the Scriptures say it.

In the first chapter, we looked at Isaiah 66:1, where the Lord said that the heavens are His throne. As you read these Scriptures, you will begin to understand that God's throne is much bigger than a conventional throne sitting in some palace room. We talked about the scepter, which is God's symbol of authority. We talked about Pharaoh, in Genesis 41:38-40. In any kingdom, the greatest level of authority is always on the throne. Pharaoh said, "Joseph, you're going to be equal with me. I'm going to give you my ring. You will be equal with me—*except when I am on the throne.*" So the throne is where the highest level of authority is.

Living Beings in Scripture: Cherubim and Seraphim

Let's look at some of the living beings and creatures in Scripture. Who or what are they? According to Scripture, they are bodyguards. God guards His holiness. And if God Almighty guards His holiness, how much more do you and I need to guard ours? There are people I avoid before I'm going to minister. There are phone calls I will not take. I won't allow people to download any problems on me right before I'm going to preach. I learned years ago not to allow negative thoughts or attitudes to enter my soul.

This is revelation that I didn't get from any human. God revealed this to me directly. In this chapter, we'll be dealing with high level angels—*cherubim and seraphim.* The Hebrew word for seraphim literally means "burning ones." That's a seraphim's purpose: to burn. We're also going to look at the living creatures in the book of Revelation, chapters 4 and 5.

If you go to Ezekiel 1, you'll find living creatures. By the time you get to Ezekiel 10, you'll discover that Ezekiel refers to them as *cherubim.* The living creatures in Revelation 4 and 5 are never called anything but living creatures. They don't have wheels, but they have six wings. The living creatures in Ezekiel 1 and 10 have four wings. The living creatures in Revelation 4 and 5 have one head each. The living creatures in Ezekiel 1 and 10 have four faces each. Every direction is another face. They've got eyes in every direction. Why is that? So they don't miss anything. Nothing gets past them. No one who's unholy gets past them. Their job is to guard the holiness of God.

When Adam and Eve missed it in the garden, in Genesis 3:24, "*He drove out the man; and He placed cherubim to the east of the Garden of Eden, and a flaming sword which turned every way, to guard the way to the tree of life.*" Why did God immediately have to get the first human beings out of the Garden after they had sinned? Because if Adam and Eve had partaken of the Tree of Life, as sinners, they would have forever lived in sin. So God prevented that from happening, by driving them out of the Garden and placing cherubim to guard the tree.

Let's look at Psalm 18. Here we find David in a terrible situation. Verse 4 states, "*The pangs of death surrounded me. And the floods of ungodliness made me afraid. The sorrows of Sheol surrounded me.*" Have you ever been there? "*The snares of death confronted me. In my distress, I called upon the Lord, and cried out to my God. He heard my voice from His temple, and my cry came before Him, even to His ears. Then the earth shook and trembled. The foundations of the hills also quaked and were shaken because He was angry.*" God was concerned when David got into trouble. And He's concerned when we get into trouble. He's no respecter of persons.

"*Smoke went up from His nostrils, and devouring fire from His mouth; coals were kindled by it. He bowed the heavens also, and came down With darkness under His feet. And He rode a cherub, and flew; He flew upon the wings of the wind.*" God has not been sitting around in a Throne Room for thousands of years, like I once thought. David was in trouble and he cried out to God. His life was in danger. And God got on a cherub and bowed the heavens: He got angry and came down to rescue him!

Let's look at Ezekiel 1. This is what the Lord showed me. He said, "My throne is so big that I couldn't reveal it to any one human this side of heaven." Now when we get to heaven, we'll see it all. He had to show Ezekiel the bottom side. He showed Isaiah the top side, because he was high and lifted up, and the seraphim were above the throne. And he showed John the panoramic view— at eye level.

With that in mind, let's start with the bottom of the throne, Ezekiel 1, beginning with verse 1: "*Now it came to pass in the thirtieth year, in the fourth month, on the fifth day of the month, as I was among the captives, by the River Chebar, that the heavens were opened, and I saw visions of God.*" So Ezekiel is on the earth, by this particular river, and suddenly he saw all the way to the third heaven. This is not Jesus; this is the Father.

Let's go a little bit further. "*On the fifth day of the month, which was the fifth year of King Jehoiachin's captivity, the word of the Lord came expressly unto Ezekiel the priest, the son of Buzi, in the land of the Chaldeans by the river Chebar; and the hand of the Lord was upon him there. Then I looked, and, behold, a whirlwind was coming out of the north, a great cloud, and a raging fire engulfing itself; and a brightness was all around it and radiating out of its midst as the color of amber, out of the midst of the fire.*"

Ezekiel beheld the whole heavens opening before him. He saw into the third heaven. Suddenly a whirlwind appeared. Scripture tells us that God travels in whirlwinds. He came in a whirlwind to get Elijah, and He's still traveling in whirlwinds. Not a tornado—tornados are a destructive force. This is a whirlwind, which shields us from the glory of God. Why does He have to be shielded? Because if we, in these frail bodies of flesh, saw God in His fullness, we'd die. He had to hide from Moses behind the rock. Can you imagine pure living fire? That's God. He is fire. He is light. When Ezekiel saw God, He appeared in the whirlwind, coming out of the north. Not the North Pole; due north--the place I spoke of in the previous chapter that science will never find because it is the dwelling place of God. And that whirlwind was coming out of the third heaven, down to the earth. If that whirlwind will come down to the earth in Ezekiel's time, it will come down now, because God hasn't changed. If He ever changes, we're in trouble. But He's not going to change. He said, *"I am the Lord thy God; I change not."* Ezekiel saw the whirlwind coming down, *"a great cloud with raging fire engulfing itself, and brightness was all around it, and radiating out of its midst, like the color of amber out of the midst of the fire."* That wasn't a normal whirlwind: there was fire coming out of it!

"Also from it came the likeness of four living creatures. And this was their appearance: they had the likeness of a man. Each one had four faces, and each one had four wings."

Four Living Creatures: the Cherubim

Four living creatures...and this was their appearance: They had the likeness of a man. Each one had four faces. What did the living creatures in Revelation 4 and 5 have? Each had one face, and six wings. These living creatures each had four faces and four wings. Obviously, they are not the same. Ezekiel didn't know they were cherubim at that time. He didn't find that out until chapter 10.

Let's read on from verse 7:

"Their legs were straight, and the soles of their feet were like the soles of calves' feet. They sparkled like the color of burnished bronze. The hands of a man were under their wings on their four sides; and each of the four had faces and wings. Their wings touched one another. The creatures did not turn when they went, but each one went straight forward.

As for the likeness of their faces, each had the face of a man; each of the four had the face of a lion on the right side, each of the four had the face of an ox on the left side, and each of the four had the face of an eagle. Thus were their faces. Their wings stretched upward; two wings of each one touched one another, and two covered their bodies. And each one went straight forward; they went wherever the spirit wanted to go, and they did not turn when they went. . As for the likeness of the living creatures, their appearance was like burning coals of fire, like the appearance of torches going back and forth among the living creatures. The fire was bright, and out of the fire went lightning. And the living creatures ran back and forth, in appearance like a flash of lightning. Now as I looked at the living creatures, behold, a wheel was on the earth beside each living creature with its four faces."

Let's pause right there and go back to Daniel 7, starting with verse 9. *"I watched till thrones were put in place, and the Ancient of Days"*—God the Father—*"was seated. His garment was white as snow, and the hair of His head was like pure wool. His throne was a fiery flame, and its wheels a burning fire."*

This was a revelation to me! I had thought that God the Father was "up there" for thousands of years, sitting on His throne, never coming down. But He began to show me something different in His word. We've got solid Scripture to back it: The throne's got wheels!

"The appearance of the wheels and their workings was like unto the color of beryl, and all four had the same likeness. The appearance of their workings was, as it were, a wheel in the middle of a wheel. When they moved, they went toward any one of four directions; they did not turn aside when they went. As for their rims, they were so high they were awesome; and their rims were full of eyes, all around the four of them. When the living creatures went, the wheels went beside them; and when the living creatures were lifted up from the earth, the wheels were lifted up"

This big entourage had come down. It hit the earth, and then it went upwards and came back down to earth again. Ezekiel watched as these wheels went up with the living creatures and came down, but he still hadn't seen God. What he observed was the bottom side of how God travels.

Back to verse 20: *"Wherever the spirit wanted to go, they went, because there the spirit went; and the wheels were lifted together with them, for the spirit of the living creatures was in the wheels. When those went, these went; when those stood, these stood; and when those were lifted up from the earth, the wheels were lifted up together with them, for the spirit of the living creatures was in the wheels.*

The likeness of the firmament above the heads of the living creatures was like the color of an awesome crystal, stretched out over their heads. And under the firmament their wings spread out straight, one toward another. Each one had two which covered one side, and each one had two which covered the other side of the body. When they went, I heard the noise of their wings, like the noise of many waters, like the voice of the Almighty, a tumult like the noise of an army; and when they stood still, they let down their wings. A voice came from above the firmament that was over their heads; whenever they stood, they let down their wings."

Why do we need the throne to come down into our lives? Because God speaks from His throne. In the next verse, Ezekiel hears a voice. He still hasn't seen God, but he hears Him speak. We're going to hear God speak from His throne, and it's going to change the whole course of things in this country.

Verse 25: *"A voice came from above the firmament that was over their heads; whenever they stood, they let down their wings. And above the firmament over their heads was the likeness of a throne, in appearance like a sapphire stone; on the likeness of the throne was a likeness with the appearance of a man high above it. Also from the appearance of His waist and upward I saw, as it were, the color of amber with the appearance of fire all around within it; and from the appearance of His waist and downward I saw, as it were, the appearance of fire with brightness all around. Like the appearance of a rainbow in a cloud on a rainy day, so was the appearance of the brightness all around it. This was the appearance of the likeness of the glory of the Lord. So when I saw it, I fell on my face, and I heard a voice of One speaking."*

Anytime the fire and glory fall, God will speak. We're going to learn how to get the throne to come in. When the throne's here, the only voice you'll be hearing is God's. First Corinthians

14 says there are many voices in the land, and none of them are without signification. That's why there's so much confusion in the church of the living God—because we've got too many voices coming in. But He's only got one voice--and we need His throne and His fire and His glory! We need to hear His voice.

Do you want to know how the church is going to become one? It's not going to be through doctrine. The five-fold ministry caused a unity of the faith, but it didn't say there would be one flock through it. I'm going to show you in the Bible how the one flock is going to manifest before His return. And that's every color, every creed, every background, every ethnicity, and every social status.

John 10:14 says, *"I am the good shepherd, and I know My sheep, and am known by My own. As the Father knows Me, even so I know the Father; and I lay down My life for the sheep. And other sheep I have which are not of this fold; them also I must bring, and they will hear My voice; and there will be one flock and one shepherd."*

That's how it will happen: We've got to hear the one voice. Just His. When the throne's present, that's all there is....And that's all that matters.

CHAPTER 3
MORE ON EZEKIEL'S VISION

This study on God's throne is the most powerful revelation that God has ever given me, and the revelation is growing. We found in the last chapter that cherubim carry the throne. God's throne moves: it's not fixed in one place called "the Throne Room." It has wheels of fire, and each cherubim has one of the wheels.

Let's return to Ezekiel 1:25: "*A voice came from above the firmament that was over their heads; whenever they stood they let down their wings. And above the firmament over their heads was the likeness of a throne.*" As we have seen, there are three views of the throne in Scripture: this throne is so big that God could not reveal it, in its entirety, to any one human being. He gave Ezekiel the bottom view. He gave Isaiah the top view. And he gave John the eye-level view. So get it out of your head that God's throne is in a room that you must enter. That's not Scripture. We've looked at Scripture that tells us that heaven is God's throne. Here, in Ezekiel 1, it says "*Above the firmament over their heads was the likeness of a throne, in appearance like a sapphire stone.*" Sapphire is blue, which represents the hottest color of fire. And so upon the likeness of the throne was a likeness of a man higher up. "*Also from the appearance of His waist and upward I saw, as it were, the color of amber with the appearance of fire all around within it; and from the appearance of His waist and downward I saw, as it were, the appearance of fire with brightness all around. Like the appearance of a rainbow in a cloud on a rainy day, so was the appearance of the brightness all around it. This was the appearance of the likeness of the glory of the Lord."*

The cherubim carry the glory. They guard it. *"So when I saw it I fell on my face and I heard a voice of One speaking."* And so you see there are times that people will fall. If God doesn't move on you to fall, then don't fall. If God's moving on you to fall and you resist, then you resist the anointing in you. You've got to go with how God's moving on you. That's the key. Many times people will fall, just like Ezekiel—he fell on his face. You've got to go with how God is moving.

Ezekiel 2: *"And He said to me, 'Son of man, stand on your feet, and I will speak to you.' Then the Spirit entered me when He spoke to me, and set me on my feet; and I heard Him who spoke to me. And He said to me: 'Son of man, I am sending you to the children of Israel, to a rebellious nation that has rebelled against Me.'"*

The Spirit of God spoke to me and said, "There's a parallel between what I spoke to Ezekiel, concerning the house of Israel, and what I am speaking to the United States of America." We could say God has sent us to the United States of America, the rebellious nation. God has sent me as a prophet, to the United States of America, to a rebellious nation "that has rebelled against Me," God says. "They and their fathers have transgressed against Me to this very day, and they are impudent." That means without shame. Every commercial you see, every program, it seems like people are saying, "How much more clothing can I shed in front of everybody? How many acts of adultery and fornication can I put in a show?" You can't go to a department store without young girls trying to show as much of their bodies as possible, trying to get somebody to look at them. That's impudent—without shame. This nation has come to a place that is without shame. Therefore, God is raising up prophets that will cry and speak "thus sayeth the Lord." For they are impudent and stubborn children. Im telling you, God spoke to me as clearly as I've ever heard Him, and there's a parallel for this, and the United States of America. "I am sending you to them and you shall say to them, 'thus says the Lord God.'"

"And you, son of man, do not be afraid of them nor be afraid of their words, though briers and thorns are with you and you dwell among scorpions." There are scorpions in this nation.

"Do not be afraid of their words or dismayed by their looks, though they are a rebellious house. You shall speak My words to them, whether they hear or whether they refuse, for they are rebellious."

Where did all this come from? It came after he saw the cherubs and the throne and the Father, when the fire falls and the cherubs come and the throne lands... And later you will learn how you can get God's throne to come to your house. You *can* get it to come to your house. You can get it to come to any service, where we get into a certain realm, and we're going to learn what realm that is, scripturally. It says His throne moves. Why does it move? It's looking for a place worthy of it. What is God doing? He's driving that throne and He's telling the cherubs where to go; He's looking for a people worthy of it dropping down on. Oh, I want it here!

The same fire that will cause a real move of God one place will also bring judgment to others. That's why you're seeing a good old thing happening to Ezekiel. You may say to me, "Are you afraid. Brother Darrell?" Certainly not! The fear of man brings a snare; the fear of the Lord is the beginning of wisdom. If you fear the Lord, you'll fear no man. Just let one of those people, who don't like what God's doing, get close to one of those cherubim—they won't last even a second. Their life will be gone, over, done.

"But you, son of man, hear what I say to you. Do not be rebellious like that rebellious house; open your mouth and eat what I give you.' Now when I looked, there was a hand stretched out to me; and behold, a scroll of a book was in it. Then He spread it before me; and there was writing on the inside and on the outside, and written on it were lamentations and mourning and woe."

Ezekiel 3 continues: *"Moreover He said to me, 'Son of man, eat what you find; eat this scroll, and go, speak to the house of Israel,' [or as we could say, the United States of America], so I opened my mouth, and He caused me to eat that scroll. And He said to me, 'Son of man, feed your belly, and fill your stomach with this scroll that I give you.' So I ate, and it was in my mouth like honey in sweetness.*

Then He said to me: 'Son of man, go to the house of Israel and speak with My words to them. For you are not sent to a people of unfamiliar speech and of hard language, but to the house of Israel, not to many people of unfamiliar speech and of hard language, whose words you cannot understand. Surely, had I sent you to them, they would have listened to you. But the house of Israel will not listen to you, because they will not

listen to Me; for all the house of Israel are impudent and hard-
hearted. Behold, I have made your face strong against their
faces, and your forehead strong against their foreheads. Like
adamant stone, harder than flint, I have made your forehead;
do not be afraid of them, nor be dismayed at their looks, though
they are a rebellious house.'

Moreover He said to me: 'Son of man, receive into your heart
all My words that I speak to you, and hear with your ears. And
go, get to the captives, to the children of your people, and speak
to them and tell them, "Thus says the Lord God," whether they
hear, or whether they refuse.'

It is time that God is raising up prophetic voices in this
nation, whether they hear or whether they refuse. And the
Lord is giving me revelation about how these fires are going to
happen today. It's in Ezekiel. I'm telling you, I feel like God's
just been downloading from heaven into my spirit.

"Then the Spirit lifted me up, and I heard behind me a great
thunderous voice: "Blessed is the glory of the Lord from His place!"

You see all of this is going on, and the cherubim are still
present, because the glory's there. Even when judgment comes,
the cherubim are present, because they carry the glory—the
same glory that's going to revive part of this nation and is
going to bring judgment to others. It'll be the same glory, the
same throne, the same cherubs and the same fire.

I also heard the noise of the wings of the living creatures that
touched one another, and the noise of the wheels beside them,
and a great thunderous noise. So the Spirit lifted me up and
took me away, and I went in bitterness, in the heat of my spirit;
but the hand of the Lord was strong upon me. Then I came to

*the captives at Tel Abib, who dwelt by the River Chebar; and I
sat where they sat, and remained there astonished among them
seven days. Now it came to pass at the end of seven days that
the word of the Lord came to me, saying, 'Son of man, I have
made you a watchman for the house of Israel.'"*

God says, too, as a parallel, "I have made you a watchmen
for the United States of America. Therefore, hear a word from
My mouth and give them warning from Me." So I'm giving
warning right now that wherever this message goes, you are
getting a warning from the Lord Himself.

Now turn to Ezekiel chapter 9. *"Then He called out in my
hearing with a loud voice, saying, 'Let those who have charge over
the city draw near, each with a deadly weapon in his hand.' And
suddenly six men came from the direction of the upper gate,
which faces north, each with his battle-ax in his hand. One man
among them was clothed with linen and had a writer's inkhorn
at his side. They went in and stood beside the bronze altar."*

What's on top of the cherubim? The throne. And Who sits
upon it? The Father. And He›s the One giving all the orders.
*"Now the glory of the God of Israel had gone up from the cherub,
where it had been, to the threshold of the temple. And He called
to the man clothed with linen, who had the writer›s inkhorn at
his side; and the Lord said to him, 'Go through the midst of the
city, through the midst of Jerusalem, and put a mark on the
foreheads of the men who sigh and cry over all the abominations
that are done within it.' To the others He said in my hearing,
'Go after him through the city and kill; do not let your eye spare,
nor have any pity. Utterly slay old and young men, maidens
and little children and women; but do not come near anyone on
whom is the mark; and begin at My sanctuary."*

Has God changed? Absolutely not. And He)s not going to. God says the first thing He's going to do is to clean house, starting with the pulpit. Those who have spoken lies and are declaring that they are God's chosen when they are not, judgment will surely strike there first. *"So they began with the elders who were before the temple. Then He said to them, 'Defile the temple, and fill the courts with the slain. Go out!' And they went out and killed in the city. So it was, that while they were killing them, I was left alone; and I fell on my face and cried out, and said, 'Ah, Lord God! Will You destroy all the remnant of Israel in pouring out Your fury on Jerusalem?' Then He said to me, 'The iniquity of the house of Israel and Judah is exceedingly great, and the land is full of bloodshed, and the city full of perversity; for they say, The Lord has forsaken the land, and the Lord does not see! And as for Me also, My eye will neither spare, nor will I have pity, but I will recompense their deeds on their own heads.' Just then, the man clothed with linen, who had the inkhorn at his side, reported back and said, 'I have done as You commanded me.'"*

Let's look at chapter 10: *"And I looked, and there in the firmament that was above the head of the cherubim, there appeared something like a sapphire stone, having the appearance of the likeness of a throne. Then He spoke to the man clothed with linen, and said, "Go in among the wheels, under the cherub, fill your hands with coals of fire from among the cherubim, and scatter them over the city." And he went in as I watched. Now the cherubim were standing on the south side of the temple when the man went in, and the cloud filled the inner court. Then the glory of the Lord went up from the cherub, and paused over the threshold of the temple; and the house was filled with the cloud, and the court was full of the brightness of the Lord's glory. And the sound of the wings of the cherubim was heard even in the outer court, like the voice of Almighty God when He speaks.*

"As for their appearance, all four looked alike--as it were, a wheel in the middle of a wheel. When they went, they went toward any of their four directions; they did not turn aside when they went, but followed in the direction the head was facing. They did not turn aside when they went. And their whole body, with their back, their hands, their wings, and the wheels that the four had, were full of eyes all around. As for the wheels, they were called in my hearing, "Wheel." Each one had four faces: the first face was the face of a cherub, the second face the face of a man, the third the face of a lion, and the fourth the face of an eagle. And the cherubim were lifted up. This was the living creature I saw by the River Chebar. When the cherubim went, the wheels went beside them; and when the cherubim lifted their wings to mount up from the earth, the same wheels also did not turn from beside them. When the cherubim stood still, the wheels stood still, and when one was lifted up, the other lifted itself up, for the spirit of the living creature was in them. Then the glory of the Lord departed from the threshold of the temple and stood over the cherubim. And the cherubim lifted their wings and mounted up from the earth in my sight. When they went out, the wheels were beside them; and they stood at the door of the east gate of the Lord's house, and the glory of the God of Israel was above them. This is the living creature I saw under the God of Israel by the River Chebar, and I knew they were cherubim. Each one had four faces and each one four wings, and the likeness of the hands of a man was under their wings. And the likeness of their faces was the same as the faces which I had seen by the

River Chebar, their appearance and their persons. They each went straight forward."

This is a large portion of Scripture, but I feel it is needed to lay a further foundation, as we delve into this book on God's throne. I love how each cherub is in charge of one of the wheels of the throne: When the cherubim went, the wheels went beside them, and when the cherubim lifted up their wings to mount up from the earth, the wheels did not turn from beside them. When the cherubim stood still, the wheels stood still. And when one was lifted up, the other lifted itself up, for the spirit of the living creatures was in them.

In the next chapter, we'll look at some of John's revelation from God.

CHAPTER 4

EZEKIEL'S VISION CONTINUES: THE FALL OF LUCIFER

In the last chapter we discussed the realm of the cherubim and their role of carrying the throne and the glory of God, and we touched upon how it's going to bring a move of God in this nation, as well as judgment upon the United States of America.

Now let's look at Exodus 25:22. You know that God gave Moses instructions to construct a type of what's in heaven (the tabernacle), but it's just a type, and it represents coming into communion with the Almighty: *"And there I will meet with you, and I will speak with you from above the mercy seat."* The throne in heaven is far above the mercy seat, just as when Ezekiel was looking up above their heads through the firmament and saw the throne, and the shape of a man upon it--God the Father, whose voice he heard emanating from the throne. And that's where this scripture in Exodus says God would speak: above the mercy seat in between the two cherubim upon the ark of the testimony where *"everything which I will give up in commandment to the children of Israel."*

There is additional scripture that we need to consider in this chapter, concerning the impending judgment of this nation, and that scripture is in the book of Ezekiel. Let's review a bit: Cherubim have four wings. And the living creatures around the throne—the seraphim—have six. We will reinforce this truth throughout this book, so that you'll know it backwards and forwards.

That's why the living creatures around the throne cannot be the same as the ones in Ezekiel. They don't have the same number of wings. Another difference: the beings around the throne have one face each. And each one is a different face. The cherubim beneath the throne have four faces; every direction is a face.

Now let's look at Ezekiel 13, beginning with verse 1: "*And the word of the Lord came to me, saying, 'Son of man, prophesy against the prophets of Israel who prophesy, and say to those who prophesy out of their own heart, 'Hear the word of the Lord!' Thus says the Lord God: 'Woe to the foolish prophets, who follow their own spirit and have seen nothing! O Israel, your prophets are like foxes in the deserts.'*"

In the last chapter I mentioned that the Lord has spoken concerning a parallel in the book of Ezekiel between Israel and the United States of America. There are many people going around, calling themselves prophets in this country. The Lord says we can say to the United States of America, your prophets are like little foxes in the deserts.

"*You have not gone up into the gaps to build a wall for the house of Israel to stand in battle on the day of the Lord. They have envisioned futility and false divination, saying, 'Thus says the Lord!' But the Lord has not sent them; yet they hope that the word may be confirmed.*"

What does this sound like? Turn over to Mathew 7:14: "*Narrow is the gate and difficult is the way which leads to life, and there are few who find it.*"

Remember, heaven will not get an inch bigger, but hell has enlarged itself. That's the reality of hell. Beware of false prophets who come to you in sheep's clothing. A false prophet is not what many people think. A false prophet is someone who is prophesying in the name of the Lord. There are a lot of people prophesying these days. A friend of mine was in a conference recently, and there were a number of people in attendance that called themselves apostles and prophets. But when my friend stood up to speak, those so-called prophets moved backwards, one of them almost to the very back of the room. Why? They weren't all speaking from the Lord. Beware of false prophets who come to you in sheep's clothing. They look like Christians. They smell like Christians. They talk like Christians. They act like Christians. But they're not Christian. Inwardly, they are ravening wolves. You will know them by their fruit. They will not gather grapes from thorn bushes or figs from thistles.

Skip down to verse 22: *"Because with lies you have made the heart of the righteous sad, whom I have not made sad; and you have strengthened the hands of the wicked, so that he does not turn from his wicked way to save his life. Therefore you shall no longer envision futility nor practice divination; for I will deliver My people out of your hand, and you shall know that I am the Lord. "*

Back to Ezekiel 13, verse 6: *"They have envisioned futility and false divination, saying, 'Thus says the Lord!' But the Lord has not sent them; yet they hope that the word may be confirmed. Have you not seen a futile vision, and have you not spoken false divination? You say, 'The Lord says,' but I have not spoken."*

They're using the Lord's name! So how will you know if a spoken "thus says the Lord" is from God or from man? You will need to know the voice of God. You will need to have your

Word level up to determine whether or not the Lord has actually spoken, to test what's coming forth from the mouths of those who claim to be His prophets.

"Have you not seen a futile vision, and have you not spoken false divination? You say, 'The Lord says,' but I have not spoken. Therefore thus says the Lord God: 'Because you have spoken nonsense and envisioned lies, therefore I am indeed against you,' says the Lord God. My hand will be against the prophets who envision futility and who divine lies; they shall not be in the assembly of My people, nor be written in the record of the house of Israel, nor shall they enter into the land of Israel. Then you shall know that I am the Lord God."

Verse 10: *"Because, indeed, because they have seduced My people, saying, 'Peace!' when there is no peace..."*

Whom have they seduced? The world? No, Satan's got them. The false prophets have seduced the church. The church has allowed false prophets into their assemblies, saying, *peace.* I can tell you what they are prophesying: It's all about money. "Peace and prosperity are coming!" Indeed they have seduced God's people, proclaiming a false peace. It doesn't matter what name they go by; names mean nothing to God if He didn't send them.

God also mentions—and warns against-- false prophetesses. Verse 17: *""Likewise, son of man, set your face against the daughters of your people, who prophesy out of their own heart; prophesy against them."*

Troubled days are coming, but God will provide for all those who hear His voice! God will work miracles for you! Those who hear the voice of the Lord, God will supernaturally manifest and move through you in this hour!

Let's look at the judgment that's coming to the false shepherds, as recorded in the book of Ezekiel: judgment upon those who have set themselves up in a pastoral office and are not called of God. They are business people, who desire to make money, to manipulate people and to gather a crowd. The world's largest gathering of people will be religious, and the one who will head it will be called the False Prophet.

The one world church is being formed right now. In many seminaries of the main denominations, people are being trained to accept Buddhism—to accept everybody. But real Christians don't want that; we have no room for that. There are men and women standing in front of thousands of people in various congregations, and they are not called of God. Many of them are lost and will split hell wide open.

That's a bitter pill to swallow, but it's the truth. I like what it says in Ezekiel 33:33: *"And when this comes to pass--surely it will come--then they will know that a prophet has been among them."*

Let's look at Ezekiel chapter 34: *"And the word of the Lord came to me, saying, 'Son of man, prophesy against the shepherds of Israel, prophesy and say to them, Thus says the Lord God to the shepherds: 'Woe to the shepherds of Israel who feed themselves! Should not the shepherds feed the flocks? You eat the fat and clothe yourselves with the wool; you slaughter the fatlings, but you do not feed the flock. The weak you have not strengthened, nor have you healed those who were sick, nor bound up the broken, nor brought back what was driven away, nor sought what was lost; but with force and cruelty you have ruled them.'"*

There are ministers, raking in millions of dollars today,

who stand behind pulpits asking for money, while people attending their churches are struggling. God will require an answer from those false shepherds. It may shock you, when God begins to expose just who these false shepherds are.

Look at verse 8: " '*As I live,*' *says the Lord God,* '*surely because My flock became a prey, and My flock became food for every beast of the field, because there was no shepherd, nor did My shepherds search for My flock, but the shepherds fed themselves and did not feed My flock*'-- *therefore, O shepherds, hear the word of the Lord! Thus says the Lord God:* '*Behold, I am against the shepherds, and I will require My flock at their hand; I will cause them to cease feeding the sheep, and the shepherds shall feed themselves no more; for I will deliver My flock from their mouths, that they may no longer be food for them.*' "

Let's turn, now, to Isaiah 14:12-14. Satan used to be a cherub--the highest of all cherubim. "*How you are fallen from heaven, O Lucifer, son of the morning! How you are cut down to the ground, you who weakened the nations! For you have said in your heart:* '*I will ascend into heaven, I will exalt my throne above the stars of God; I will also sit on the mount of the congregation on the farthest sides of the north; I will ascend above the heights of the clouds, I will be like the Most High.*' *Yet you shall be brought down to Sheol, to the lowest depths of the Pit.*"

Ezekiel 28 also talks about Lucifer: "*Moreover the word of the Lord came to me, saying,* '*Son of man, take up a lamentation for the king of Tyre, and say to him, Thus says the Lord God: You were the seal of perfection, Full of wisdom and perfect in beauty. You were in Eden, the garden of God; every precious stone was your covering: The sardius, topaz, and diamond, beryl, onyx, and jasper, sapphire, turquoise, and emerald with gold.*

The workmanship of your timbrels and pipes was prepared for you on the day you were created. You were the anointed cherub who covers; I established you; you were on the holy mountain of God; you walked back and forth in the midst of fiery stones. You were perfect in your ways from the day you were created, till iniquity was found in you.'"

Let's look at the last part of verse 13. *"The workmanship of your timbrels and pipes was prepared for you on the day you were created."* That word translated "tabrets or timbrels" is the Hebrew word *toph*. It means "small drums." It was the common instrument of percussion in ancient times. In other words, Lucifer, the anointed cherub, was in charge of music. He had drums inside his being. He didn't have to play them; they played themselves. When he was in charge of the praise and worship in the holy mountain of God, he walked on the fiery stones. He was given his own throne to head up that ministry. And he said it was not good enough. "I am going to be like the Most High. I will exalt my throne above the stars of God." And when God cast him down, he took a third of the angels with him. He's been after music on this planet ever since. That's why there are so many secular rock groups that are drawing our young people into hell. Because Lucifer still has the beat. When God gives a gift, He never takes it back: it is there, but the anointing is gone. Music is good; rhythm and beat are good. God gave Lucifer those drums, and now this fallen angel is trying to pull millions into the pit with him with that gift. That's why Satan hates anyone leading praise and worship, because they have taken his place. He can never go up the mountain of God again, nor walk on the stones of fire.

My oldest son was caught up in Lucifer's beat, and what

happened to him is connected with sound and music. He ran from God and anything to do with my wife and me. One particular Sunday, he purchased a pistol and was going to pick it up from the gun shop and use it to blow somebody away. At that time, he frequently drove through drug dealings in a big city. Here's an anointed man of God's son, driving around, trying to get killed, robbing drug dealers and hoping he would die. That's a classic story of somebody running from God.

One day, however, he slipped in the back door of the church service. The Lord said to me, "Today, I want you to deal with the number 27, the number of rock stars that die at 27-- Hendrix, Joplin, you'll find a long list." Every person that had the charisma to reach the masses had a call of God on them; and because they were called and rejected it, they got into trouble and died young. I believe there's a special place in hell just for people who refused to preach the gospel when God had called them to do just that.

My son was in the back of the church during the service. He was 26 at the time, but the Holy Ghost said, deal with 27 today. I didn't even know what He meant, but He said deal with the number; and when I did, God got through to my son. He never shot anyone that day. He never got the pistol he had purchased. The power of God told him, "That's you--you're preparing to die. You're going to be just like one of those 27-year-olds." The power of God then pulled my son to the front of the church and got him to his knees. Demons were in him. He told me later he felt like going off on everybody, with all the rage that was in him. But the power of God stopped him and dropped him to his knees. God said, "Now, look, you can go down this way, or I'm going to put you on your face." God pulled him to his knees, and he came to Jesus. Jesus freed him from demons, filled him with the Spirit, and he accepted the call to preach.

Sometime later, he was preaching to the young people in the youth room, and he asked them, "How many of you know ICP (Insane Clown Posse)?" All the young people in that room raised their hands. ICP is just one of many groups that's sending our young people to hell, because they've got Lucifer's beat. What kind of beat is in your house? What kind of CDs, what kind of channels, what kind of doors are you opening up in your home? Oh, but they're young. It's okay. Just give them three or four years. If that is your attitude, you may be attending your son's or daughter's funeral, if you don't put a stop to it.

The devil is after your kids. Every time you play a CD, you are releasing sound waves that have been frozen in time, and whatever is captured on that CD-- if there were demons that were invoked in the recording--they have a right to operate again. If the anointing of the Holy Spirit was captured in that recording, it will release the power of God every time.

Just as the cherubim usher in the glory of God, so the fallen cherub, now known as Satan, ushers in the presence of evil through music, through sounds. What are you going to allow in your home? What are you going to allow for yourself, or for your children?

CHAPTER 5

THE VISIONS OF ISAIAH AND JOHN

This book concerns the revelation that God has given me about His throne. There are seven fires before the throne that we're going to look at. Every one of them is a flame with a specific anointing. God wants you to experience all seven of these fires.

God's throne is so big that He couldn't give the complete view to any human this side of heaven. We know that Ezekiel saw the bottom part of God's throne, and Isaiah saw the top view. Let's look at Isaiah 6 beginning with verse 1: "*In the year that King Uzziah died, I saw the Lord sitting on the throne, high and lifted up. And the train of His robe filled the temple.*" Notice the keys to each of these views. In Ezekiel, the prophet is looking up, while the throne descends from heaven. That is why he saw the cherubim and all of that which carries it, including the wheels. Each cherub has one wheel.

In Isaiah, this prophet of God gets a view of what's above the throne—and there stood the seraphim. There are no cherubim here. God has order. He has specific angelic beings that carry out specific tasks. The cherubim don't speak. They aren't crying, "Holy, holy, holy." What are they doing? They're protecting the fire. And they've got eyes in the rims of the wheels. They're looking at anything that even tries to get near God. If you're not holy, you won't make it. You'll die. If something unholy crosses that threshold, it's dead.

Remember the rebellious prophet, Balaam, who was motivated by money. God said to him, when he had agreed to curse the Israelites, "Don't go." But he kept going. Balaam discovered what happens when a rebellious prophet persists in going against God. God spoke through the prophet's donkey: He gave that donkey a human voice! The donkey was more spiritual than that rebellious prophet, because he saw that God had set an angel with a flaming sword right in front of them. If Balaam had crossed that threshold, he would have been killed, just like that. But the donkey prevented that from happening.

And that's what those angelic beings are all about: beneath the throne, around the throne, above the throne, they're fire. If anything ungodly tries to cross the threshold, it is destroyed instantly.

So we know that Isaiah, in his vision, saw another type of being: the Seraphim, which in Hebrew means "burning one." While the cherubim carry the fire, in between their wheels, the seraphim have to go get it.

"Above it stood the seraphim." Notice the direction: *above* the throne, and note, also, that there are places to stand. Walking, or standing, in heaven is not like walking or standing on the earth. Rather, it's multi-dimensional. Remember that Heaven is 1,500 miles high. To be honest, I don't know how high the throne is from top to bottom. The Bible doesn't tell us. But it must be huge. Ezekiel, who's looking up at the wheels on the bottom of the throne, notices that the rims are high. Imagine the top view, with the seraphim looking at it, all the way down to the wheels—that will give you a better idea of what the throne will look like when we see it. It's sure to be phenomenal!

The seraphim stand above God's throne. *"Each one had six wings: with two he covered his face, with two he covered his feet, and with two he flew. And one cried to another and said, 'Holy, holy, holy is the Lord of Hosts. The whole earth is full of His glory.' And the posts of the door were shaken by the voice of him who cried out. And the house was filled with smoke. So I said, 'Woe is me'"*

Who is this saying, *"Woe is me?"* It is none other than Isaiah, a powerful prophet. But in the presence of God, he felt unclean. The stronger the presence of the Lord, the more we'll be looking at ourselves in this manner. "Lord, is there anything wrong with me?" That's a good thing. I was in a meeting one time and the conviction power was very strong. Suddenly this girl screamed and ran out of the meeting, because she wasn't willing to deal with herself. That was one of the saddest things I remember. God was convicting her; it was so strong. But she refused to yield; thus, she went screaming out of the meeting.

"So I said, 'Woe is me, for I am undone! Because I am a man of unclean lips, and I dwell in the midst of a people of unclean lips; for my eyes have seen the King, the Lord of Hosts.' Then one of the seraphim flew to me, having in his hand a live coal which he had taken with the tongs from the altar."

The cherubim all have an assignment: they can get the coals, because they have them. The seraphim, we have learned, do not. Notice what the seraphim have to do: *"The seraphim flew to me. He had in his hand a live coal, which he had taken with the tongs from the altar."* The seraphim cannot get the coals with their hands. They have to use tongs. And once they get the coals, then they're able to take them wherever God sends them.

"Then one of the seraphim flew to me, having in his hand a live coal which he had taken with the tongs from the altar. And he touched my mouth with it, and he said: 'Behold, this has touched your lips; your iniquity is taken away, and your sin purged.' Also I heard the voice of the Lord saying, 'Whom shall I send, and who will go for us?'"

Notice that he distinguishes iniquity from sin. Iniquity is the weakness in your life that keeps sin at your door. It's what pulls you into sin. Iniquity is a flaw. When the iniquity is gone, the sin will be gone. Take, for example, somebody who committed adultery. The adulterer asks the Lord to forgive him, but next week, the sin returns. The Bible talks about the sin that so easily besets us. If you have iniquity, you can't break away from that same old sin. Until the iniquity is gone, you're going to keep falling into that sin, over and over again.

Let's look at that verse again. *"Behold, this has touched your lips. Your iniquity is taken away."* Why did the seraphim take away the iniquity first? So Isaiah wouldn't keep sinning. He removed the iniquity, and then he said, *"And your sin [is] purged."* In other words, it is finished and you won't fall into that sin again.

Notice verse 8. When Ezekiel saw the bottom of the throne, he heard the Voice. Isaiah saw the top of the throne, and he heard the Voice. Why do we need the throne to come into our midst? When the throne is present, there's only one Voice we'll hear: the Voice of God. What does 1 Corinthians 14 say? Many voices in the land. None of them are without signification. And that's why we need the throne—it's God's own Voice.

"Also I heard the voice of the Lord saying, 'Whom shall I send?'"

Right here and now, He's asking that of us: *"Whom shall I send, and who will go for us?"* Who will go to a city that needs to hear My Word? God is asking us that today. *"Then I said, 'Here am I, send me,' and He said, 'Go, and tell this people.'"*

Let's go to Revelation 1:4. As we have discovered, John was given the panoramic eye-level view, all around. The key word is *around*. What was the key word in Isaiah? *Above*. And the key word in Ezekiel? *Beneath*. Ezekiel saw the throne coming down. He was looking at the *bottom*. Three different views altogether.

"John, to the seven churches which are in Asia. Grace to you and peace from Him who is and who was and who is to come, and from the seven Spirits who are before His throne." The *Amplified Bible* says, *"John, to the seven assemblies (churches) that are in Asia. May grace (God's unmerited favor) be granted to you and spiritual peace (the peace of Christ's kingdom) from Him who is and Who was, and Who is to come, and from the seven Spirits [the seven-fold Holy Spirit] before His throne."*

There is a seven-fold Holy Spirit. That's why God gave instruction to Moses to make the menorah, beaten out of one piece of gold—a seven-branched candlestick, because there's one Holy Spirit, with seven fires.

Let's go back to Revelation 1: *"I was in the Spirit on the Lord's Day, and I heard behind me a loud voice, as of a trumpet, saying, 'I am the Alpha and the Omega, the First and the Last,' and, 'What you see, write in a book and send it to the seven churches which are in Asia: to Ephesus, to Smyrna, to Pergamos, to Thyatira, to Sardis, to Philadelphia, and to Laodicea.' Then I turned to see the voice that spoke with me. And having turned I saw seven golden lampstands."*

I'm not going to expound on this portion of Scripture in detail: this is not a teaching on the seven churches. But I want us to take a look at the first church, because there is a revelation here about what makes a church a church. It's certainly not the name. It's certainly not the sign. It's not the carpet—or lack of it. The answer to this question is found in the letter to the very first church: *"To the angel of the church of Ephesus write, 'These things says He who holds the seven stars in His right hand, who walks in the midst of the seven golden lampstands: "I know your works, your labor, your patience, and that you cannot bear those who are evil. And you have tested those who say they are apostles and are not, and have found them liars; and you have persevered and have patience, and have labored for My name's sake and have not become weary. Nevertheless I have this against you, that you have left your first love. Remember therefore from where you have fallen; repent and do the first works, or else I will come to you quickly and remove your lampstand from its place--unless you repent.'"*

This church was given many commendations. One of them has to do with the Ephesian church's ability to spot imposters in their midst. Just because someone shows up saying he's a prophet, that doesn't mean you just accept it—give him the test. This church knew how to test those claiming to be apostles. It says, *"You have tested those who say they are apostles and are not, and have found them liars. And you have persevered and have patience and have labored for my name's sake, and have not become weary."*

The Ephesian believers had all this in their favor. But the passage goes on to say, *"Nevertheless, I have this against you: You've left your first love."* What's the remedy? *"Remember therefore from where you have fallen."* This church had already fallen. *"Repent and do the first works or else I will come to you quickly and remove your lampstand from its place, unless you repent."*

What makes a church a church is that the Lord Jesus Christ has placed His lampstand there. That's why there's fire; that's why there's anointing; and that's why, when believers gather together, He's ever-present, because He's placed His lampstand in the midst of them. But when the Lord removes His lampstand from a place, there may be ten thousand people coming every Sunday, but it is no longer a church. It's a social club, a feel good club. But it is not a church.

There's a "sad news commentary" concerning the church at Ephesus. If you trace its history, the Ephesian church never repented, and to this day, there's not a move of God in the area where this church was located. God removed His lampstand. Let that never be said of our churches, or of anyone that is following the Lord. When God shows us an area in which we need to repent, let us quickly repent, and keep following the Lord.

Let's look at Revelation 4, starting with verse 1. Now we're going to get a panoramic, eye-level view of God's throne: *"And the first voice which I heard was like a trumpet speaking with me, saying, 'Come up here, and I will show you things which must take place after this.'"* You can be sure that when the throne comes into your house, you're going to hear the Voice of the Lord. And you won't go astray when you hearken to His Voice.

"Immediately I was in the Spirit; and behold, a throne set in heaven, and One sat on the throne. And He who sat there was like a jasper and a sardius stone in appearance; and there was a rainbow around the throne, in appearance like an emerald. Around

the throne were twenty-four thrones, and on the thrones I saw
twenty-four elders sitting, clothed in white robes; and they had
crowns of gold on their heads. And from the throne proceeded
lightnings, thunderings, and voices. Seven lamps of fire were
burning before the throne, which are the seven Spirits of God."

Those seven fires are burning right now. We're going to
look at scripture concerning those fires. God revealed to me
that He's going to release those fires on those hungering and
thirsting after Him.

"Seven lamps of fire were burning before the throne, which are
the seven spirits of God." Those seven fires are mentioned in
Isaiah 11:1-2. This is prophecy of the Lord Jesus. *"There shall*
come forth a Rod from the stem of Jesse, and a Branch shall
grow out of his roots. The Spirit of the Lord shall rest upon him."

SEVEN FIRES OF THE SPIRIT OF GOD:
The Spirit of the Lord
The spirit of wisdom
The spirit of understanding
The spirit of counsel
The spirit of strength
The spirit of knowledge
The spirit of the fear of the Lord

Notice which one He places emphasis upon in verse 3:
"His delight is in the fear of the Lord." In other words, He said,
"That's the fire that is more important than all of rest—the
fear of the Lord." This highlights what we'll be looking at later
on in this book.

As we discussed earlier, if you've got any kind of iniquity--If
you've got any kind of a weakness toward any type of sin, God

says there's a coal from the altar that will free you, just as the seraph brought the purifying coal to Isaiah.

Let's look at Revelation 4, verse 5 again: *"And from the throne proceeded lightnings, thunderings, and voices. Seven lamps of fire were burning before the throne, which are the seven Spirits of God [the seven-fold Holy Spirit]."* Verse 6: *"Before the throne there was a sea of glass, like crystal. And in the midst of the throne, and around the throne, were four living creatures."*

Are these living creatures the cherubim? Let's look at the description once again: The four living creatures *"were full of eyes, in front and in back. The first living creature was like a lion, the second living creature like a calf, the third living creature had a face like a man."*

Notice the difference between these living creatures and the cherubim: The cherubim each have four faces. These living creatures, however, are never given any specific designation. They don't have a wheel, and each has one face, and every living creature looks different.

"And the fourth living creature was like a flying eagle. The four living creatures, each having six wings." Earlier we learned that the cherubim have four wings, which sets them apart as different. *"The four living creatures, each having six wings, were full of eyes around and within. And they do not rest day and night, saying: "Holy, holy, holy."* According to the Scriptures, the cherubim do not speak. But the seraphim do. And these living creatures also speak. They say, *"'Holy, holy, holy, Lord God Almighty, who was and is and is to come!' Whenever the living creatures give glory and honor and thanks to Him who sits on the throne, who lives forever and ever, the twenty-four*

elders fall down before Him who sits on the throne and worship Him who lives forever and ever, and cast their crowns before the Lord, saying: 'You are worthy, O Lord, to receive glory and honor and power; for You created all things, and by Your will they exist and were created.'"

As we complete this chapter, I'd like to share a personal revelation with you. Just a few years ago, God began to change everything about me. One day when I came into my office, preparing to enter into the worship that was already going on, the Lord spoke to me. He said, "Son, there's all kinds of Christian music today. Every kind of style is out there." Then He said, "Why not find out what I like?" That shook me! The Lord brought me to Revelation 4 and when I went out into that service, I read that passage of Scripture. It began to change everything in my life. God said, "If you want throne level anointing, then find out what lyrics I like. They are "Holy, holy, holy. Worthy, worthy, worthy." Much of the music that is sung during worship services is "outer court" music. I said, "No! I don't want outer court, Lord! I want to be at your throne!"

How about you? Do you want to be at His throne? Remember, the highest level of authority is at the throne. The highest level of the anointing is at the throne. The highest level of the glory is at the throne. Psalm 103:19 (AMP) says, *"The Lord has established His throne in the heavens, and His kingdom rules over all."* Maybe you have some things in your life that are not being ruled over by God. God is calling you closer, saying, "Come to My throne. Stand at My throne, and watch My kingdom rule over all."

CHAPTER 6
ACCEPTING OUR ASSIGNMENTS FROM GOD

L et's now look at 1 Corinthians 3, beginning with verse
7: *"So then neither he who plants is anything, nor he who
waters."* That means there is no big "I" or little "you" in the
kingdom. There are no big shots in the kingdom. There was
a problem in the Corinthian church. Some were aspiring to
become big shots, and there were cliques forming. So Paul had
to straighten it out. He said, "He who plants and he who waters
are equal—of the same importance and esteem. Yet each shall
receive his own reward, wages, according to his own labor."

God records everything. Every work you do after Christ is
recorded: how it was done and why it was done. This thought
keeps me sober. It's even recorded if the Lord actually called
you to do the work you're doing. There are people pastoring
churches today that God never called. They were called to make
money, to fund the gospel. So everything that's been done by
them will be burned by the heavenly fire, because they never
were true pastors. They were more like businessmen, running
big businesses. Rather than feeding the people, they sucked the
people dry, and rolled in the millions of dollars they amassed
in the process. They may have titles and material possessions,
but there's no call of God upon their lives.

In my forty-plus years of ministry, I experienced a one-
year period when I tried to leave the ministry. I was pastoring
in a town in east Texas, preaching on the different kinds of

prayer—prayer of intercession, prayer of agreement, prayer of petition—and they all have different rules. I was demonstrating what I was preaching to my people. One day, I had my kick-boxing clothes on, my belt and everything. Kick-boxing was something I did with my kids, on a regular basis. I even won a couple of trophies. But I had a "he-man" mentality, and I wasn't satisfied. I thought, I'm going to have to pump iron. I'm going to have to increase the weights and the squats. Nothing was enough. I worked and worked until one day, I popped a right inguinal hernia. That will take any kind of self-exaltation out of you quickly!

I was pastoring at this time and I had just gotten my last bit of ministerial abuse, as a result of my attempt to be "he-man." I was on my way to the emergency room, hobbling, and a parishioner was following me, trying to get some last minute counseling. A miracle of healing did not happen at that time. My injury was the direct result of my own stupidity, so I had to learn from it. But I was frustrated and hurting, so I said, "That's it! I resign!" However, you can't just resign from what God has called you to do. And if you're doing something God has not called you to do, it's best to say, "God, I'm sorry, I repent! I will do what You called me to do." What you will answer for, one day, is the assignment—and whether you did it or not.

You may be in some kind of school right now. Or you may be a teacher. Have you ever had to be responsible for an assignment? If you missed a day at school, did it change your assignment? Not likely! When you get to class and your name is called, either you'll have the assignment done or there will be consequences.

When you stand before God, as a Christian, the very first

issue to be discussed is your assignment. Don't bother lamenting, "It was too hard! The people were too stubborn and contrary." That won't hold water with God. Jeremiah dealt with hard people. Isaiah dealt with hard people. And Ezekiel dealt with hard people. Assignments aren't always easy.

In my attempt to evade my assignment, I said, "God, I just want to be a good deacon. Just let me be a good deacon somewhere. I know how not to give the pastor any problems. I know how to pray for the pastor. I know how to be a faithful tither. I'll be a model church member." I felt a weight coming off of me—I was certain that God was going to allow me to be a church member!

We ended up at a church north of Austin, Texas. Somebody had set us up in a nice house. They said, "We'll take care of all the bills, etc." Then all of that fell through. The owner called me for eviction. An F-5 tornado, 260 miles an hour, ripped through Gerald, Texas, leaving a number of people dead in its wake. The winds were so strong, that it pulled the grass up out of the ground. Suddenly, the F-5 split into two or three F-3s. After it turned over a train, knocking it off the tracks, it ripped through a supermarket, collapsing it in the middle. Then it made a right turn and headed straight for our subdivision!

My two girls were swimming at the pool. Our youngest son was a little baby at the time. All of a sudden the girls heard an announcement that everybody needed to get out of the pool and go home. They didn't know the severity of it—the tornado was just minutes away and headed in our direction; I have never seen a tornado that close. That funnel cloud was aimed at our house; the debris cloud was just above my head. On the front porch everything was spinning. The whole block was chaotic. And our neighbors were from the north; they didn't know what to do.

God will have mercy whether you're in His perfect or permissive will. God had mercy for Jonah when he ran from his assignment. And I was a Jonah then. While everything was spinning around us, my wife was saying to the neighbors, "Go in your houses, we will take care of it." That's the very first time I spoke to a storm, and we commanded it to go exactly where we wanted it to go. Our only precedent for storms is in the Scriptures: to speak to them, not to pray about them. Jesus spoke to the storm. And He said we would do the works that He did and greater, because he was going to the Father. That F-3 tornado turned and went exactly where we pointed. We shut the door and went inside the house, and kept waiting and waiting. Nothing happened. The storm passed by and our block was saved.

Then, as if that weren't enough, we ended up moving to the Houston area. We got to the area at about two in the morning and discovered that there had been a tragic murder on my wife's side of the family. Husband and wife—in a Spirit-filled church together, the Sunday before. I questioned, "How much of God's Spirit was in that church?" A word of knowledge would have discerned and prevented that tragedy. But instead, a murder had been committed.

All of this took place in the year that I decided to leave the ministry. When God calls you to an assignment, it will never change. You will answer for that assignment: you cannot circumvent it, because it is not your choice. You do not choose your assignment—you discover it.

Many people become jealous over assignments: One can sing like an angel, for instance, while another can't carry a tune in a bucket. But remember that God equips you for your particular assignment. You've got all that you need to carry out God's will for your life.

Let's go to 1 Corinthians 3:10: *"According to the grace of God which was given to me, as a wise master builder I have laid the foundation, and another builds on it. But let each one take heed how he builds on it..."* Grace is the special endowment for your task--or your assignment. That's why a shy little boy named Darrell—who is still shy, and really doesn't like to be around a lot of people—can be called to preach. There are people who are shocked when they're around me in regular life, because I don't talk a lot. I like to spend my time talking and listening to God, and if I'm in a conversation with somebody, I want to hear what they're saying.

In James it says, *"Be quick to hear, slow to speak, slow to get angry."* We've got two ears and one mouth. That seems to indicate that we should be listening twice as much as we are talking!

Back to 1 Corinthians 3:10: *"According to the grace of God which was given to me, as a wise master builder I have laid the foundation, and another builds on it. But let each one take heed how he builds on it. For no other foundation can anyone lay than that which is laid, which is Jesus Christ."*

Can you change the foundation? No, but you can build something upon it. However, just because the foundation is solid, doesn't mean that what you're building upon it is. *"Now if anyone builds upon the foundation with gold, silver, precious* stones, wood, hay..." According to this portion of Scripture, not everything that is built upon the foundation endures. What does fire do to wood and hay? It burns them up. *"...each one's work will become clear; for the Day will declare it, because it will be revealed by fire; and the fire will test each one's work, or what sort it is."* Where's that fire? In front of the throne: the seven purifying fires of the Spirit of God. They're burning right now. They'll never stop burning. It's impossible to come to the throne without passing through those seven fires. This thought keeps me humble; it keeps me sober; and it keeps me from never, ever trying to resign from the ministry again. No matter how hard, no matter how tough, no matter how many don't like me, I will never, ever walk away from my assignment again.

"And it will be revealed by fire; and the fire will test each one's work, of what sort it is." The fire won't just appraise the work; it will appraise the character, also.

When your work is being judged, you won't be able to say, "But it was that woman You gave me." Or, "Oh, I'd do it, Lord, if I wasn't married to him." What does it say here? *". . . and the fire will test each one's work, of what sort it is. If anyone's work which he has built on it endures, he will receive a reward. If anyone's work is burned, he will suffer loss; but he himself will be saved, yet so as through fire. Do you not know that you are the temple of God and that the Spirit of God dwells in you? If anyone defiles the temple of God, God will destroy him. For the temple of God is holy, which temple you are."*

So why not let the barn burn down? I say it quite regularly: "God, anything You don't want in me, take it out of me. I don't want it. I don't have time for it." You don't have time for it, either.

If you're reading this, you may have a call of God on your life and are currently running from it. You may say, "I don't really know my assignment; but I want to know." Or perhaps the Lord has dealt with you about an area of ministry, but you have resisted getting involved in it. Now is the time to go all the way with what He's called you to do.

CHAPTER 7

THE SEVEN FIRES OF GOD

G od downloaded this revelation to me, straight from heaven. God shut me up for fourteen years out in the country, out in a small place, and He downloaded revelation knowledge to me and released me as a prophet to the nations. And one of the revelations He gave me was about His throne--that it moves. We've gone through this, chapter by chapter, verse by verse. Don't take any teaching from me or anybody else, unless you see it in God's word.

We've looked in depth beneath the throne. We've looked in depth above the throne. And we've looked in depth around the throne, and discussed the twenty-four elders and the seven fires that are in front of the throne—the sevenfold Holy Spirit. And each of those flames is constantly burning. We discovered in the last chapter, for Christians, that we can either experience the fire of God now and let it burn up everything in our lives that is not of Him, or when we stand before the judgment seat of Christ, we'll cross those fires, and any work that's not of Him will be burned up then. I choose to let it burn now. How about you?

Now we're at the point of identifying those seven fires. In Revelation 1:4 (Amp), it says, *"John to the seven assemblies (churches) that are in Asia: May grace (God's unmerited favor) be granted to you and spiritual peace (the peace of Christ's kingdom) from Him Who is and Who was and Who is to come, and from* the seven Spirits [the sevenfold Holy Spirit] before His throne."

Let's look at Revelation 4:5 (Amp): "*Out from the throne came flashes of lightning and rumblings and peals of thunder, and in front of the throne seven blazing torches burned, which are the seven Spirits of God [the sevenfold Holy Spirit]*."

In the last chapter we discussed the menorah. Why did God give such specific instructions for that sevenfold candlestick? It had to be hammered out of one piece of gold, because there's only one Holy Spirit, yet the Spirit has seven flames.

The Seven Flames:

Those seven flames are identified in Isaiah 11, beginning with verse 1 (NASB): "*Then a shoot will spring from the stem of Jesse, and a branch from his roots will bear fruit. The Spirit of the Lord will rest on Him.*"

The first flame: The spirit of the Lord

The second flame: the spirit of wisdom.

The third flame: the spirit of understanding.

The fourth flame: the spirit of counsel.

The fifth flame: the spirit of strength.

The sixth flame: the spirit of knowledge.

The seventh flame: the spirit of the fear of the Lord.

"*And He will delight in the fear of the Lord.*"

Nine Hebrew Words for Praise

I had eight Hebrew words for praise, but the Lord added a ninth. Every Hebrew word for praise is different—each word means a specific expression of praise. Let's look at them together:

1. *Yadah: Yadah* means to open and extend your hands to God. It is used in Psalm 54:1-7. The word *praise* in that passage is *yadah.*

2. *Towdah*: It means to extend the hands with thanksgiving or gratitude. That's used in Psalm 100, when we enter his gates with *towdah.*

3. *Shabach*: This word is used in Psalm 63:1-3 (NASB). It means to address in a loud tone. When God says to go up and praise Him, He used this particular word. That's why to praise Him specifically will give you a specific result. *"O God, You are my God; I shall seek You earnestly; my soul thirsts for You, my flesh yearns for You, in a dry and weary land where there is no water. Thus I have seen You in the sanctuary, to see Your power and Your glory. Because Your lovingkindness is better than life, my lips will praise [shabach] you."*

4. *Barak*: It means to kneel, and it also means to bless. In Psalm 103, David was commanding his soul to bless the Lord. Your mind, will, and emotions may not feel like blessing Him at times. That's why you have to learn to command it. *"Bless the Lord, O my soul, and all that is within me, bless His holy name. Bless the Lord, O my soul, and forget not all His benefits: who forgives all your iniquities, who heals all your diseases, who redeems your life from destruction."*

5. *Shachah*: In Psalm 95:6, *"Oh come and let us worship,"* *shachah* means to stretch out prostrate before the Lord. It also means to fall down before the Lord, to crouch, to humbly beseech, to reverence, and to worship. We've got two powerful words in this one scripture. "Oh come and let us *shachah*, and let us *barak*—kneel."

6. *Zamar*: It means to touch the strings, to play upon an instrument. Most people who sing purchase an accompaniment track: a track of pre-recorded music to sing to. But *zamar* means to make music that is accompanied by the voice. In other words, *zamar* refers to an anointed musician who, through prayer and worship, gets hold of heavenly music and brings it down to earth. And then God provides a voice to accompany the music. That's how prophetic singing takes place. The word *zamar* is found in Psalm 108:1-2.

7. *Ruwa:* It means to mar by breaking, to split the ear with sound. In Joshua 6:16, when God said to march around the walls of Jericho for seven days, then seven times on the seventh day, the word he used for shout was *ruwa.* If the Israelites had not split the ear with sound, the walls would not have come down, because that was the command of God: to shout with a loud voice.

8. *Halal*: This word means to be a fanatic, to rant, to be clamorously foolish for the Lord. It is used in Psalm 22:22; and, again, in Psalm 34:2, where it says, *"My soul shall make her boast in the Lord."* Halal is where the word *hallelujah* comes from. It's the combination of two Hebrew words, *halal* and *Yah. Yah* is the Hebrew word for God. There are times in Scriptures when God says, *"Halal* me." That's what David was doing when his wife Michal made fun of him. And God cursed her and shut her womb. If you're ashamed of God, then don't expect Him to be excited about you, either.

9. *Tehillah:* This indicates the place when you get beyond merely praising the Lord and begin to access His praise. *Tehillah* comes from halal. Many times you must halal your way to *tehillah.* You can literally jump start a move of God

with *halal*. You'll find in Scripture that the halal preceded the tehillah, as it was with Jehoshaphat, because tehillah is the only kind of praise that God is obligated to enthrone. Where is the highest level of authority in His kingdom? The throne. We've already seen that the throne moves throughout the heavens. It is looking for those who enact *tehillah*. It's looking for a group in *tehillah*, so it can enthrone that level of praise. When that happens, miracles will take place. Psalm 103 (Amp) says, *"The Lord has established His throne in the heavens, and His kingdom rules over all."* Is sickness included in "all"? Is divorce included in "all"? Financial problems? *"His kingdom rules over all."*

Let's look at several verses where the word *tehillah* is used;

Deuteronomy 10:20-21: *"You shall fear the Lord your God; you shall serve Him and to Him you shall hold fast and take oaths in His name. He is your praise [tehillah] and He is your God, who has done for you these great and awesome things which your eyes have seen."* *Tehillah* is directly related to miracles. If we can only get out of programmed praise. People come into worship services with all kinds of problems and difficulties. So it's good to have some structure, to focus on the Lord. But at some point, what God wants every single time we meet, is for us to get into *tehillah*. And when we do, His throne will come in on top of that praise. And when His throne comes in, that's when miracles happen.

Deuteronomy 26:18 says, *"Also today the Lord has proclaimed you to be His special people, just as He promised you, that you should keep all His commandments and that He will set you high above all nations which He has made, in praise [tehillah]."* The Spirit of the Lord will release a mantle of *tehillah* that you can wear, in which His throne will inhabit you and your house.

In 2 Chronicles 20, the concept of *tehillah* completely changed this whole story for me. I've read it; I've heard it preached. What was the word of the Lord to Jehoshaphat when the enemy gathered against him? Let's start at verse 18: *"Jehoshaphat bowed his head with his face to the ground, and all Judah and the inhabitants of Jerusalem bowed before the Lord, worshiping the Lord. Then the Levites of the children of the Kohathites and of the children of the Korahites stood up to praise the Lord God of Israel, with voices loud and high."* God wanted the *halal* there.

"So they rose early in the morning and went out into the Wilderness of Tekoa; and when they went out, Jehoshaphat stood and said, 'Hear me, O Judah and you inhabitants of Jerusalem: Believe in the Lord your God, and you shall be established; believe His prophets, and you shall prosper.' And when he had consulted with the people, he appointed those who should sing to the Lord and who should praise [halal] the beauty of holiness." There were specific people who were to *halal*--probably those who were the most radical.

"As they went out before the army and were saying, 'Praise the Lord, for His mercy endures forever." Here is *yadah* again. But He still didn't send the ambushments.

"Now when they began to sing . . ." Here is the word *tehillah*, which indicates that they got out of merely praising Him, and suddenly accessed His praise, the praise of heaven. Psalm 22:3 began to manifest, and God enthroned their praise. *"But You are holy, enthroned in the praises of Israel."* He is *enthroned* (*yashab*) upon the *tehillah*. *Yashab* means to sit down, to sit

down as judge, to sit down in ambush, to sit down in quiet, to remain, to dwell, to marry, and to enthrone. In other words, when God enthrones your tehillah praise, He will be sitting on His throne upon that praise to be whatever you need Him to be at the moment. If you've been dealing with a situation, God will judge it for you, if you get into *tehillah*. When the Israelites began to sing, the Lord set ambushes. When they got away from their efforts to simply praise and began, rather, to access His praise, *"The Lord set ambushes against the people of Ammon, Moab, and Mount Seir, who had come against Judah; and they were defeated."*

And this is the word of the Lord to all of us. No matter what you're facing, no matter what the doctor's report, no matter who's allied against you, you can be overcomers, if you will push past the *yahdah*; if you will push past the *towdah;* if you will push past radically praising him in the *halal* and the *shabach* and the *zamar....* The Scripture says, *"I waited for the Lord, for His praise,"* not my praise. Why are we waiting? Lord, we're doing what we know to do. We're praising, we're lifting our hands, but God, what we're waiting for is Your praise to arrive, and then Your throne will come down. And when it comes down, kingdom authority will drive out sickness and disease and demons and poverty and lack and all the enemies who have come against You.

When that happens, you don't have to fight. When that happens, you don't have to push. The push was to get into God's realm, God's reign. Once it arrives, let it take over.

CHAPTER 8

The First Fire: The Spirit of the Lord

L et me ask you a question: Whether you like who's in the Oval Office or not, if you had an appointment on a certain date and time to meet the President of the United States, would you go in every day clothes, like you were going to the mall or to visit a friend? No? And why not? Because of the office!

Who is God the Father? Jesus? The Holy Spirit? We would get dressed up to meet the President. We would change some of our behaviors to meet the Queen of England. Yet, that fire is missing in the church. The fire of the fear of the Lord is most often not to be found.

If we look once again in the book of Revelation, chapter 1, verse 4, John writes: *"To the seven churches which are in Asia: Grace to you and peace from Him who is and who was and who is to come, and from the seven Spirits, who are before His throne."*

These seven churches are types, and every one of them is has a representation operating somewhere in the world today. A lot of the churches in America are Laodicean churches. They have their increase with goods, they feel like they're prospering, and they have made the statement, "I have need of nothing." And the Lord's word to them—and to you—is this: "You're wretched; you're poor. Basically, you're spiritually bankrupt." He said, "I'd rather you were hot or cold." I used to wonder, why hot or cold? If you're cold you want to get warm. But luke-warm? If you like lukewarm coffee, bless you, but I can't stand it. When I want a cup of coffee, I want it hot. When I want some hot chocolate, I want it hot. Lukewarm is not good. If you're lukewarm, you'll fall asleep. That's why the apostle Paul wrote in a message to the church, "Awake, you who are sleeping. Arise from the dead." He wasn't saying that to the world—he was writing to a church that should have been red hot for God. Awake! And so I say to the American church, Awake! Awake and arise from the dead. Get out of your lukewarm slumber and become red hot. Get one of those coals from God's altar.

This entire message to the seven churches came from the One who is, and who was, and who is to come, and from these seven fires. The seven fires—or seven spirits—were involved in the message that came.

Go with me to Revelation 4:5. It says, *"And from the throne proceeded lightnings, thunderings, and voices. Seven lamps of fire were burning before the throne, which are the seven Spirits of God..."* And those seven blazing torches are burning right now, the seven Spirits of God—the seven-fold Holy Spirit.

The *tehillah* praise is the only kind of praise that the Lord's throne is going to come upon. And when it comes, those seven fires will be there, because they are ever before the throne. We have looked at a number of Scriptures in which *tehillah* was the word used for *praise.* Let's look at Psalm 34, starting with verse 1: "I will bless the Lord at all times." Notice the depth that's in this one verse. To bless him at all times does not mean to bless him all the time. I will bless him at all times. In other words, good times, bad times, you can do that. But the next part of the verse, "His praise shall continually be in my mouth,"—it's impossible for *halal* to continually be in my mouth, because I can't radically be jumping around praising Him 24/7.

What does *halal* mean? To be a fanatic in your praise. That's what King David was doing when his wife Michal, Saul's daughter, made fun of him. And God cursed her for mocking: He closed her womb—she never had a child, because she made fun of David's praise. So don't criticize the way someone else praises God. It's beautiful in the sight of the Lord.

We discussed the Hebrew word *yadah* in a previous chapter. It means to extend the hands. You can't do that 24/7, either. But what word is used in Psalm 34:1? *Tehillah*. His *tehillah* shall continually be in my mouth. You are doing the blessing, and *tehillah* occurs when you've accessed His own praise. You no longer have to push into it. Now, He's there. In other words, God wants us to get to the place where there's a constant flow of His praise—not ours—coming out of us, like gushing rivers of water, to a place where His throne can just reside. To where we can literally walk every day in His presence.

Let's look at Psalm 40, starting with verse 1: *"I waited patiently for the Lord; and He inclined to me, and heard my cry. He also brought me up out of a horrible pit, out of the miry clay, and set my feet upon a rock, and established my steps. He has put a new song in my mouth."* This is not me, praising Him. Do you see the difference? He has put the song into me. Why was He waiting for that moment? He was waiting for *tehillah*.

Have you ever wondered why David was so anointed? Why could David come into the presence of King Saul, who was troubled by an evil spirit, and begin to play the harp and sing? Because he knew how to wait on the Lord. He knew how to wait until *tehillah*—God's praise—arrived. He understood that when God's praise comes down, all struggling ceases. Until that happens, until we reach that point of revelation, we do whatever we need to do. We *halal*, we *yadah*, we lift our hands, we sing, we press in. But there comes a moment when that divine flow descends into our midst. And once that happens, there's no longer pressing, no longer striving. That's when His praise has become our praise.

"He has put a new song in my mouth." That "new song" has never been played before—at least not on the earth. There are innumerable songs in heaven right now. They're waiting for musicians and singers to press into the Lord long enough to get one. That requires patience and perseverance. And that's the problem in the U.S. today: we've become a microwave society. We've got a drive-through mentality. Two minutes is too long to wait. There are even drive-through churches! The problem is, the throne isn't going to come in on that. You're going to have to wait on the Lord. Before a service, I'm waiting on Him—for hours and hours, waiting on Him. What am I doing while I'm waiting? I'm praying in the spirit; I'm worshiping; I'm doing what I know to do until He shows up. *Tehillah* praise is when His praise arrives. And when His praise arrives, His throne will be right in the middle of it!

"He has put a new song in my mouth. Tehillah to our God." I hope you never again read the Scriptures and see only the word "praise," without finding out what kind of praise it is. The English language is one of the most ambiguous languages in the world. We say, "I love God. I love my wife. I love my dog. And I love my toy." That's vague. How in the world can your love for God, your wife, your dog, and your toy all be the same? The English language has a lot of problems. And if you're an English teacher, you know there are a lot of problems when you try to teach it. That's why the Hebrew language is much better, as is the Greek language.

In Greek there are six words for love. There's *agape*—God's love. It has nothing to do with your emotions or the way you feel about any one. Agape will cause you to get up at three in the morning, when you're exhausted, and go fix somebody's tire. Agape sees the value in a person, no matter what. *Phileo* love is friendship. It's based on likes and dislikes. *Storge* is affection. Affection is based on your feelings. It's based on your emotions. *Epithumia* is a strong impulse, longing, or desire, and can be used in a positive or negative sense. *Philadelphia* is a love that can only occur between Christians. And then there's *eros*, which is pure physical attraction between a man and a woman. In order for a marriage to work, you need all six kinds of love. *Agape* should be at the top. *Storge* will fail; affection will fail. *Epithumia* will also fail; if not guarded by Agape, it will turn into lust. *Philadelphia* will fail. *Phileo* will fail; friendship will fail. *Eros*—sex—will fail. But *agape* will never fail. Because God is *agape*. *Agape* is personified—it is God Himself.

Let's look at the Hebrew word *shalom*. The Hebrew language is one of the most concise languages. It takes a good-sized paragraph in English to say what that one Hebrew word says. *Shalom* means wholeness, soundness, safety, prosperity, Divine health. It means nothing lacking and nothing broken or destroyed in your life. It means freedom from catastrophe and no beneficial thing withheld. It's the most complete word you can say to your brother or sister in the Lord. From head to toe, God's blessings and protection on you and yours. That's why this word *tehillah* is hard to put into English. It's God's own praise coming into you.

Go with me to Psalm 51, starting with verse 15. *"Oh, Lord, open my lips and my mouth shall show forth Your praise [tehillah]."* When you're in that realm, it's no longer a struggle. Praise is just flowing out; God is actually opening your lips and filling your mouth. It is the place of complete surrender to the Holy Spirit.

Psalm 71, beginning with verse 6 says, *"By you I have been upheld from birth; You are He who took me out of my mother's womb. My praise [tehillah] shall be continually of You. I have become as a wonder to many, but You are my strong refuge. Let my mouth be filled with Your praise [tehillah] and Your glory all the day."* *Tehillah* can stay in you all day long. That's God's design—for *tehillah* to be in your heart and in your mouth 24/7. Go to verse 13: *"Let them be confounded and consumed who are adversaries of my life. Let them be covered with reproach and dishonor who seek my hurt. But I will hope continually, and I will praise [tehillah] You yet more and more."*

Let's consider one more chapter and verse—Psalm 106:2: *"Who can utter the mighty acts of the Lord? Who can declare all His praise [tehillah]?"* His, not yours. The answer is, nobody can. It's too much. How can one person declare it when there's no limit to it? There's no end to it, as there is no end to God. Do you realize God doesn't live in eternity? Eternity lives in God. Eternity means there's no beginning and no end. God doesn't live in that—eternity lives in Him. He's the one who created eternity. God doesn't live in time—time lives in God. That's why when you get in the *tehillah* realm, you lose track of time.

God created time. In Genesis we read, *"In the beginning..."* And there will be a moment when time will end. There will never be time again. It'll just be God. We'll be with Him, and

He with us, on and on. We'll never need to sleep: the new bodies we'll receive will never have need of rest. There'll be no night in the New Jerusalem.

Verse 12: *"Then they believed His words; they sang His praise [tehillah]." Tehillah* belongs to God. Let's look at verse 47—this is even more personal: *"Save us, O Lord our God, and gather us from among the Gentiles, to give thanks to Your holy name, to triumph in Your praise [tehillah]."* When you get into *tehillah,* you will always triumph.

Now let's go to 1 Samuel 16, beginning with verse 11: *"And Samuel said to Jesse, 'Are all the young men here?' Then he said, 'There remains yet the youngest, and there he is, keeping the sheep.' And Samuel said to Jesse, 'Send and bring him. For we will not sit down till he comes here.' So he sent and brought him in. Now he was ruddy, with bright eyes and good-looking. And the Lord said, 'Arise, anoint him. For this is he.'"*

God will sometimes anoint one who seems the most unlikely. The Apostle Paul said, "Consider your calling." Find out what God is saying. *"'Arise, anoint him; for this is the one!' Then Samuel took the horn of oil and anointed him in the midst of his brothers; and the Spirit of the Lord came upon David, from that day forward."*

Turn to Isaiah 40:13: *"Who has directed the Spirit of the Lord?"* No one directs that fire. When you get that fire, it will direct you. Who has directed the Spirit of the Lord? No one! But when you're burning with that fire, that fire will direct you. And that fire will burn anything in front of you that's not of God. That fire will create a path that didn't exist before.

Now let's look at Isaiah 61. This is the very passage that Jesus quoted in Luke 4: *"The Spirit of the Lord God is upon Me, because the Lord has anointed Me to bring good tidings to the poor; He has sent Me to heal the brokenhearted."* Christians are going to enact these works, with God's fire. We're going to bring good news to the afflicted. We're going to bind up the broken hearted. We're going to proclaim liberty to the captives. We're going to proclaim freedom to the prisoners, to proclaim the favorable year of the Lord and the day of vengeance of our God; to comfort all who mourn. To grant those who mourn in Zion, giving them a garland instead of ashes, the oil of gladness instead of mourning, the mantle of *tehillah*, instead of a heavy, burdened, failing, and fainting spirit. The first fire, the Spirit of the Lord, will put a mantle of *tehillah* on you. You may still be wondering, why do we need the mantle of *tehillah*? *"So that we will be called oaks of righteousness, the planting of the Lord, that He may be glorified."*

God once brought a message through me about being an oak tree. I studied oak trees in depth. We used to live on thirty-one acres with all kinds of oak trees: post oaks, pin oaks, live oaks. One day, quite suddenly, they all began to die. Those majestic trees had been there for years. I discovered, in my research, that in oak trees, for the first fifty or sixty years, the roots shoot down. After that, they don't go downward—they start spreading out, and they are very particular about what's around them. If something takes root by an oak that it doesn't like, the oak is affected. In similar fashion, if you, as a Christian, allow the world to dwell in your "root-space," then you'll start to wither, and spiritually you'll begin to die. We watched as one oak tree after another fell victim to this death-process. As I researched oak trees, looking for answers, I discovered that you cannot mess with their roots once they start spreading out.

God wants you to stand alone for Him. And His fire, His mantle of *tehillah* is going to enable you so that, as a mighty, majestic oak, you're not going to allow sin around you. You're not going to allow compromise around you. But you're going to be on fire for God.

Isaiah says, *"He will rebuild ancient ruins."* This anointing is going to enable you to go into ruined areas where, previously, you weren't able to do any good. But now, with this holy fire, you'll be able to go in with a fresh blaze: you're going to be wearing this mantle, and the Fire of the Spirit is going to direct you as to what to do in that region.

"They will raise up the former devastations." Some of you may have gone to places where God led you, but you didn't have this fire. But once this fire is released upon you, God is going to enable you to tear down the devastation and raise up His habitation. *"And they will repair the ruined cities."* That's prophetic. It concerns the cities around you that God says are going to be affected with this move, with this Holy Spirit Fire. He's going to enable you to go into places and repair them.

The fire of the Spirit of the Lord will release a powerful mantle upon you, so that you can be an oak of righteousness, one that will stand tall and not allow compromise in any area of your life.

CHAPTER 9

THE SECOND FIRE: THE SPIRIT OF WISDOM

In the previous chapter, we discussed the seven fires that are burning right now before the throne of God. Each one of these flames is a special anointing. In this chapter, we're going to going to look at the second fire. The first fire is the Spirit of the Lord; the second fire is the Spirit of Wisdom.

The Hebrew word for wisdom in Isaiah 11 is *chokmah.* It means intelligence. I'm not talking about expanding your brain, I'm talking about a fire that's burning right now before the throne. It can give you intellectual insight in a moment. It means special abilities, skill; it is the knowledge and ability to make the right choices at the opportune time. It means wit. It means wisdom that is ordained and created by God that is manifested in many ways in the universe that He created.

Isaiah tells us what each of the seven fires are in chapter 11, beginning with verse 1 (NASB): *"Then a shoot will spring from the stem of Jesse, and a branch from his roots will bear fruit. The Spirit of the Lord will rest upon Him, the spirit of wisdom and understanding, the spirit of counsel and strength, the spirit of knowledge and the fear of the Lord."*

So when the fire called *the spirit of wisdom* is released, it will bring with it all of these: intelligence, special abilities, skill, knowledge, and the ability to make the right choices in your life, at the opportune time, so you don't miss God moments: wit and wisdom that are ordained and created by God that are manifested in many ways throughout the universe. I want us to look at a number of scriptures concerning this wisdom.

Let's begin in the Old Testament, in Exodus 28:3: *"So you shall speak to all who are gifted artisans, whom I have filled with the spirit of wisdom."* There is a spirit of wisdom. There is an anointing to be wise.

Deuteronomy 34:9 says, *"And Joshua the son of Nun was full of the spirit of wisdom, for Moses had laid his hands on him; so the children of Israel heeded him, and did as the Lord commanded Moses."* That is the best scriptural evidence that wisdom can come from laying on of hands.

Psalm 111:10 states, *"The fear of the Lord is the beginning of wisdom."* Now the fear of the Lord is the final fire of these seven fires, and when we study the spirit of the fear of the Lord we'll find a holy awe and reverence in conjunction with it.

Proverbs 8:11-12 (KJV) tells us, *"For wisdom is better than rubies; and all the things that may be desired are not to be compared to it. I, wisdom, dwell with prudence, and find out knowledge of witty inventions."*

In the New Testament, in 1 Corinthians 1, beginning with verse 24, we read: *"But to those who are called, both Jews and Greeks, Christ the power of God and the wisdom of God. Because the foolishness of God is wiser than men, and the weakness of God is stronger than men."* Verses 30-31 go on to say, *"But of Him you are in Christ Jesus, who became for us wisdom from God—and righteousness, and sanctification, and redemption—that, as it is written, 'He who glories, let him glory in the Lord.'"*

Let's look, for a moment, at 1 Corinthians 2:6-7: *"However, we speak wisdom among those who are mature, yet not the wisdom of this age, nor of the rulers of this age, who are coming to nothing. But we speak the wisdom of God in a mystery, the hidden wisdom which God ordained before the ages for our glory."*

Verses 8 and 9 go on to say, *". . . which none of the rulers of this age knew; for had they known, they would not have crucified the Lord of glory. But as it is written: "Eye has not seen, nor ear heard, nor have entered into the heart of man the things which God has prepared for those who love Him." "*

This portion of Scripture states the things that God has prepared for us; all that He's made and keeps ready for us— you and me. He's waiting for us to apprehend them. They're available to all who love Him, who hold Him in affectionate reverence, promptly obeying Him and gratefully recognizing the benefits He has unveiled and revealed by and through His Spirit. This particular fire of the Holy Spirit searches diligently, exploring and examining everything, even the bottomless things of God. And now it says, *"But God has revealed them to us through His Spirit. For the Spirit searches all things, yes, the deep things of God."*

Now let's look at a few more verses in the New Testament:

2 Corinthians, 1:12: *"For our boasting is this: the testimony of our conscience that we conducted ourselves in the world in simplicity and godly sincerity, not with fleshly wisdom but by the grace of God, and more abundantly toward you.*

Ephesians 1:17: *"[I keep asking] that the God of our Lord Jesus Christ, the Father of glory, may give to you the spirit of wisdom and revelation in the knowledge of Him."*

Ephesians 3:7-9: *"[Through the Gospel], of which I became a minister according to the gift of the grace of God given to me by the effective working of His power. To me, who am less than the least of all the saints, this grace was given, that I should preach among the Gentiles the unsearchable riches of Christ, and to make all see what is the fellowship of the mystery, which from the beginning of the ages has been hidden in God who created all things through Jesus Christ."*

There is a realm of God's wisdom that will not be released, except it comes through you. It's complicated, all right, and many sided. What do I mean by many sided? Imagine a mountain. Somebody goes up the north side of the mountain, and they've got a whole story to tell. Somebody goes up the south side of that same mountain, and they've got a completely different story to tell. Somebody else comes up the west side of that same mountain and saw awesome things. They saw some animals nobody else saw, even though it's the same mountain. Somebody else comes up the east side, and they have a different story to tell. Then someone could go southeast or go northeast. It's all one mountain, but there are many sides. It's the same with one God. That's why His throne is too big for one human to get a complete picture of it.

We will finish with Ephesians 3:10: *"To the intent that now the manifold wisdom of God might be made known by the church to the principalities and powers in the heavenly places."*

Who is the church? I am. You are. The Greek word for

church is *ecclesia*, and it means "those who have been called out and placed into." The church is not a building. The church is those people on the planet right now who have been called out of one kingdom—darkness—and have been placed into the kingdom of light. That's the church.

This is the assignment for you and me; and when we stand before God, we will each have to answer whether or not we undertook, and completed, our assignment.

CHAPTER 10

THE THIRD FIRE: THE SPIRIT OF UNDERSTANDING

In the previous chapter, we discussed the Spirit of Wisdom.
In this chapter we're going to look at the third fire, the Spirit of
Understanding. The Hebrew word for understanding is *biynah*.
It means *the object of knowledge*. It is what a person desires
to know. How many of us desire to increase in knowledge?
Knowledge is that faculty that enables a person to answer
correctly. It is comprehension, righteous action and discernment—to be able to properly discern a situation: what is of God
and what is not? What is good and what is evil? Who is right
in this matter and who is wrong? Whose side is God on here?
It also means to perceive, to distinguish. It means insight.

Let's start in the Old Testament, looking at a number
of Scriptures:

1 Chronicles 12:32: "...of *the sons of Issachar who had understanding of the times, to know what Israel ought to do.*" We're
living in perilous times, as I write this. These are the last days.
But it takes this fire, this Spirit of Understanding, burning
upon us and through us, to correctly discern these times. If
we're relying on the newscasts for understanding, we're in
for a lot of disappointment. But this fire from heaven, which
is burning right now before the throne, will give us absolute
understanding of the days in which we live. We need to know
what to do at this particular moment in time. If great difficulties are to arise in this nation, and surely some will manifest,

we need this anointing of the third fire to know what to do—
and how best to do it.

Second Chronicles 2 (KJV), beginning with verse 12: *"Huram
said moreover, Blessed be the Lord God of Israel, that made
heaven and earth, who hath given to David the king a wise son,
endued with prudence and understanding, that might build an
house for the Lord, and an house for his kingdom."*

Job 28:28 (KJV): *"And unto man he said, 'Behold, the fear of the
Lord, that is wisdom; and to depart from evil is understanding.'"*

Proverbs 3:5 (KJV): *"Trust in the Lord with all thine heart;
and lean not unto thine own understanding."* Failure happens
when we depend upon our own understanding. That's why
we need this fire now more than we've ever needed it before.

Proverbs 4:1 (KJV): *"Hear, ye children, the instruction of a
father, and attend to know understanding."*

Proverbs 4:5 (KJV): *"Get wisdom, get understanding: forget it
not; neither decline from the words of my mouth."* Understanding
is wisdom's twin sister. They work together.

Proverbs 4:7 (KJV): *"Wisdom is the principal thing; therefore get wisdom; and with all thy getting, get understanding."*

Proverbs 9:6 (KJV): *"Forsake the foolish, and live; and go in
the way of understanding."*

Proverbs 9:10 (KJV): *"The fear of the Lord is the beginning of wisdom, and the knowledge of the holy is understanding."* God is holy.

Proverbs 16:16 (KJV): *"How much better is it to get wisdom than gold! And to get understanding rather to be chosen than silver!"*

Isaiah 29:24: *"These also who erred in spirit will come to understanding, and those who complained will learn doctrine."*

Daniel 1:20: *" And in all matters of wisdom and understanding about which the king examined them, he found them ten times better than all the magicians and astrologers who were in all his realm."*

Daniel 9:22: *"And he informed me, and talked with me, and said, 'O Daniel, I have now come forth to give you skill to understand.'"*

Daniel 10:1: *"In the third year of Cyrus king of Persia a message was revealed to Daniel, whose name was called Belteshazzar. The message was true, but the appointed time was long: and he understood the message, and had understanding of the vision."*

Now let's look at some New Testament scriptures:

Matthew 22, beginning with verse 23: *"The same day the Sadducees, who say there is no resurrection, came to Him and asked Him, saying: 'Teacher, Moses said that if a man dies, having no children, his brother shall marry his wife and raise up offspring for his brother. Now there were with us seven brothers. The first died after he had married, and having no offspring, left his wife to his brother. Likewise the second also, and the third, even to the seventh. Last of all, the woman died also. Therefore, in the resurrection, whose wife of the seven will she be? For they all had her.' Jesus answered and said to them, 'You are mistaken, not knowing the Scriptures nor the power of God. For in the resurrection they neither marry nor are given in marriage, but are like angels of God in heaven. But concerning the resurrection of the dead, have you not read what was spoken to you by God, saying, 'I am the God of Abraham, the God of Isaac, and the*

God of Jacob'? God is not the God of the dead, but of the living.'
And when the multitudes heard this, they were astonished at
His teaching."

Romans 1:28: *"And even as they did not like to retain God*
in their knowledge, God gave them over to a debased mind . . ."
What does that mean? Romans 1 says that there are no atheists.
Anyone who says there are atheists is a liar—because Romans
1 declares that there's never been a person who didn't cry out
to God, or who wasn't aware that they were going somewhere,
when they were dying. And if people profess to be atheists,
why do they use God's name in vain, especially if He doesn't
exist (to them)?

I encourage you to read all of Romans 1, in which God
declared that He has expressed Himself so clearly in all of
creation—in the stars and the moon and the sun and the trees
and the mountains and the waterfalls, and everything that
is created—that every human being on this planet knows He
exists, whether they have heard the gospel or not. God says
you're accountable for the knowledge of Himself that is revealed
throughout creation.

Once I had no answer for this question: "What about people
who haven't heard the gospel? What's God going to do with
them?" I used to just reply, "God is just," and that's all I could
say. But I have more than that now. Romans 1 says that there's
no excuse. Scripture answers Scripture, so let's go to Acts 10,
where we find a man named Cornelius. Cornelius didn't know
Jesus—or that there was even a man named Jesus. But he knew
there was a God. How did he know about God? Romans 1 says
everybody knows there's God; we carry that knowledge within
us, because creation reveals the Creator. Cornelius was trying

to get to God—doing alms, praying, being a good person.

So this is the heart of God: anybody who truly wants to know Him on planet earth, He will see to it that they hear the gospel. God sent an angel to Cornelius. The angel appeared to him and told him about a preacher. He said, "There's a man named Peter who is staying with Simon the Tanner by the sea. Go find him, and he will tell you how to get to the God you are seeking."

In the meantime, Simon Peter was having a racial problem; he didn't think that the gospel belonged to the group known as Gentiles. So God gave Peter a vision. You mean God will do all of that to get the gospel to someone who wants to know the God of Creation? Yes, indeed! That way, nobody will have an excuse on judgment day.

God gave Simon Peter a vision and showed him various kinds of foods, descending from heaven on a sheet. He said to him, "Rise and eat." Peter saw unclean foods and replied, "Not so, Lord, for I've never eaten anything that's unclean to the Jews." God said, "I've cleansed it. Don't you dare call it unclean! There's someone waiting for you." So Peter, having received this revelation that the gospel is for all people—Gentiles, as well as Jews--traveled all the way to Cornelius's home. This happened because Cornelius knew, through creation revelation, that there was a God. Romans 1 says there is no excuse.

Peter arrived at Cornelius's home and began to preach to Cornelius and all of his house--and they all got saved. They got baptized in the Holy Ghost, and all of them started speaking in tongues. Peter could not deny that salvation and the infilling of the Holy Ghost is for anyone who wants it.

Romans 1:28: *"And even as they did not like to retain God in their knowledge, God gave them over to a debased mind, to do those things which are not fitting; being filled with all unrighteousness, sexual immorality, wickedness, covetousness, maliciousness; full of envy, murder, strife, deceit, evil-mindedness; they are whisperers, backbiters, haters of God, violent, proud, boasters, inventors of evil things, disobedient to parents, undiscerning, untrustworthy, unloving, unforgiving, unmerciful; who, knowing the righteous judgment of God, that those who practice such things are deserving of death, not only do the same but also approve of those who practice them."* There's a point of no return. You can't just come to God any time you want to. The Scripture says you cannot come to the Son except the Father draws you. Somebody reading this right now may especially need to hear this truth. Let God draw you to Him, give your heart to Jesus, and let God do His will in your life.

2 Corinthians 10:12-14: *"For we dare not class ourselves or compare ourselves with those who commend themselves. But they, measuring themselves by themselves, and comparing themselves among themselves, are not wise. We, however, will not boast beyond measure, but within the limits of the sphere which God appointed us—a sphere which especially includes you. For we are not overextending ourselves (as though our authority did not extend to you), for it was to you that we came with the gospel of Christ."*

This refers to ministers who try to barge in on territory that God did not call them to. It also refers to those who say they are apostles, and try to be apostles over a work that God did not call them to. Or those who are prophets, who say that God has called them to be a prophet in a certain house, when

God never assigned them to that task. That's comparing themselves by themselves. And God says that those ministers are without understanding.

Paul continues, "*For we are not overextending ourselves (as though our authority did not extend to you), for it was to you that we came with the gospel of Christ; not boasting of things beyond measure . . .*" Those that try to force their way into an area where God did not call them are trying to boast beyond their measure. There are people who say they are apostles, and who claim to have churches; but if you talk to people in their churches, they don't claim that that person is an apostle. There are those who say they're prophets to certain places, but God is the one who sets such ministries in place.

2 Corinthians 10:15: "*Not boasting of things beyond measure, that is, in other men's labors, but having hope, that as your faith is increased, we shall be greatly enlarged by you in our sphere, to preach the gospel in the regions beyond you, and not to boast in another man's sphere of accomplishment. But 'he who glories, let him glory in the Lord.' For not he who commends himself is approved, but whom the Lord commends.*"

Ephesians 4, beginning with verse 17: "*This I say, therefore, and testify in the Lord, that you should no longer walk as the rest of the Gentiles walk, in the futility of their mind, having their understanding darkened, being alienated from the life of God, because of the ignorance that is in them, because of the blindness of their heart; who, being past feeling, have given themselves over to lewdness, to work all uncleanness with greediness.*" This is God's will for us, that the eyes of our understanding be enlightened. We can pray from Ephesians 1, "God, I am asking you to enlighten the eyes of our understanding, that we may know what is the hope of Your calling, what are the riches of Your glory of Your inheritance in the saints." Knowing the call of God for your life is connected with the enlightenment of the eyes of your understanding.

Colossians 2:2-3 says, "that their hearts may be encouraged, being knit together in love, and attaining to all riches of the full assurance of understanding, to the knowledge of the mystery of God, both of the Father and of Christ, in whom are hidden all the treasures of wisdom and knowledge."

Just from this sampling of Scriptures, we see how important it is to have understanding. Notice how much emphasis is placed, in the Bible, on being able to understand. I thank God that through His word, we can have all the understanding and the wisdom that we need.

CHAPTER 11

THE FOURTH FIRE: THE SPIRIT OF COUNSEL

In this chapter, we're going to look at the fire of the Spirit of Counsel. Our foundational Scriptures for these fires are Revelation 1:4 and 4:5

Revelation 1:4: *"John to the seven churches which are in Asia: Grace to you and peace from Him who is and who was and who is to come, and from the seven Spirits who are before His throne."*

Revelation 4:5 says, *"And from the throne proceeded lightnings, thunderings, and voices. Seven lamps of fire were burning before the throne, which are the seven Spirits of God."*

What kind of praise is it that will get God's throne to come down in our midst? *Tehillah* praise. An interesting note about music: normally, musical notes are linear. There are bars and spaces on the musical scale. When you're playing a piece of music, when you get to the end of a line, you go to the next line and so forth. That's regular music. But a musician described *tehillah* to me this way: when you move into that realm, music is no longer linear—it becomes a circle. You don't know where it started, and you don't know where it stops. There are no lines, no spaces—it moves into that never-ending realm. It is music from heaven—throne music. So *tehillah* happens when you are no longer praising. You have entered into the very praise of God, itself.

Now back to the Spirit of Counsel: The Hebrew word for

counsel in Isaiah is *etsah,* which means "counsel" or "advice." It means purpose. It means to plan. In other words, inside this fire is God's purpose for your life—or your assignment. And it's not only the purpose or assignment of God, but it is the plan to get it done.

Let's talk about our assignments for a moment. Every person in the body of Christ has an assignment, as we have previously seen. The assignment is not your decision—it's your discovery. You cannot choose your assignment. I shared with you earlier about the year I tried to leave the ministry. I became the top salesman of a company headquartered in Arkansas, trying to support my family. I thought that I could just work that kind of job, because I was tired of the ministry. As of the writing of this book, I've been in the ministry over forty years, and I can tell you, it's not easy.

This world is full of people who have tossed aside their assignments; they've gotten out of the race. But when you know that God has called you to something, and you know there's coming a day when you will stand before the Lord himself, you will each answer for what you're doing. I told God I would be such a good church member and never give anybody any trouble. The job I had taken as top salesman led me to the point where I almost bankrupted the Houston, Texas office of the company.

I was just like Jonah. There was no reason for the boat Jonah was on to have problems—except that he was on board, running from his assignment. Right now, there may be a Jonah reading this book. You may be that Jonah, running from the call of God. But you can't choose your assignment. Your assignment was chosen for you by God before you were ever in your mother's womb. And when you stand before God, you will answer for your assignment, even if you never discovered it.

I learned this truth when I was trying to be a salesman in that company: it was never going to work, because my assignment was to deliver the word of the Lord. And I will never again stop doing it.

You are not on this planet *for* a purpose. You are on this planet *because* of a purpose. And it would be a smart decision to find out what that purpose is, before you stand before God. I believe there's a special place in hell for those who were called to preach, but who rejected God. Why? Because every preacher who was called was given the charisma to reach people for Jesus. Thus, the blood of millions of souls who were never reached stains their hands, because they failed to carry out their assignments.

That's what the apostle Paul was talking about when he said, *"Necessity is laid upon me."* No choice. If I were to quit preaching—you'd see my name in the obituaries.

So do you want to be accepted? Do you want to be popular? If that's what you think is important, remember Jesus: Born in a stable. Rejected. Kicked out of the temple. And when He died, He died outside of the city. You still want to be popular? At what cost? My oldest son would give you this same testimony: How he ran from the ministry-- everything God called his mom and dad to do, he ran away from. He tried to die. He knew he was on his way to hell. The day he came back to the Lord, he didn't want to go to church, but God had his number. My son slipped in the back of the church, and God led him to repentance...and back to his assignment.

The gifts and calling of God are without repentance. That means God gives the gift, even if somebody splits hell wide open and doesn't repent. They'll have that gift with Lucifer and the beast and the false prophet, and they'll be tormented with that gift for eternity.

The assignment is not your decision. You can't say, "Well, I just want..." What you need to do is find out why you are on the planet right now. Obviously, you didn't choose to get here. The real you is not your flesh. The real you didn't come from your biological parents. The real you is a spirit, and the Father of spirits breathed your spirit inside the baby in the womb of your pregnant mom, because you needed to be here right now. He desired for you to be here now—not during the days of Jesus and the apostles; not during Isaiah's day; not during Jeremiah's day; not during Daniel's day; not during Paul's day. But right here at the end of the ages. Because there are lost people that no one will reach but you. And the Lord is asking this question: What are you going to do about it?

What is this fire of the Spirit of Counsel? It's a fire of advice. It's a fire of purpose. It's a fire of your assignment--the purpose, the assignment, and the plan to get it done. Let's look at some Scriptures concerning this particular fire:

Deuteronomy 32:28: *"For they are a nation void of counsel, nor is there any understanding in them."*

Psalm 1:1-3: *"Blessed is the man who walks not in the counsel of the ungodly, nor stands in the path of sinners, nor sits in the seat of the scornful."* You can find ungodly counsel everywhere. You can find it on the street corner. You can turn on almost any television program, and it's going to get lewder and rawer.

Godly counsel comes from meditating on the Word: "*But his delight is in the law of the Lord, and in His law he meditates day and night. He shall be like a tree planted by the rivers of water that brings forth its fruit in its season, whose leaf also shall not wither; and whatsoever he does shall prosper.*"

Let me stop here and tell you another story. I remember years ago when I lived in an apartment complex. Two kids were in their vehicle at curbside outside the complex and their music was booming—loudly. There was no place you could go in the entire complex to get away from it. It was actually shaking the doors. And those kids were extremely foul-mouthed. The Holy Ghost came on me, and I went to them and started sharing some things about life and death. I said, "Guys, I've been to all kinds of funerals. Short caskets, medium caskets, long caskets. You see, death is certain. It's appointed unto man once to die, and after that, the judgment." And I shared with them what God gave me. Then I walked away. You could see the fear of God come upon those young men. They never played another loud note the rest of the time they were there. What I gave them, the Holy Ghost burned into those two young men that night.

Psalm 73:24: "*You will guide me with Your counsel, and afterward, receive me to glory.*" It will happen just in that order. If you follow God's counsel, then there will be a day He'll receive you into His glory and His honor.

Psalm 33, beginning with verse 10: "*The Lord brings the counsel of the nations to nothing; He makes the plans of the peoples of no affect. The counsel of the Lord stands forever, the plans of His heart to all generations. Blessed, is the nation whose God is the Lord.*"

Proverbs 1:29 (this is sad): *"Because they hated knowledge and did not choose the fear of the Lord, they would have none of My counsel and despised My every rebuke. Therefore they shall eat the fruit of their own way, and be filled to the full with their own fancies. For the turning away of the simple will slay them, and the complacency of fools will destroy them."*

Proverbs 19:20: *"Hear counsel. Receive instruction and accept correction that you may be wise in the time to come. Many plans are in a man's mind, but it is the Lord's purpose for him that will stand."* You may be working on your own plans. God says they're going to fall. However, if you get hold of God's plans, things will turn around.

Proverbs 20:5: *"Counsel in the heart of man is like deep water, but a man of understanding will draw it out."*

Jeremiah 32, beginning with verse 17: *"Ah, Lord God! Behold, You have made the heavens and the earth by Your great power and outstretched arm. There is nothing too hard for You. You show lovingkindness to thousands, and repay the iniquity of the fathers into the bosom of their children after them—the Great, the Mighty God, whose name is the Lord of Hosts. You are great in counsel and mighty in work, for Your eyes are open to all the ways of the sons of men, to give everyone according to his ways and according to the fruit of his doings."*

John 14, 16-17 (Amp): Jesus said, *"And I will ask the Father, and He will give you another Comforter (Counselor, Helper, Intercessor, Advocate, Strengthener, and Standby), that He may remain with you forever—The Spirit of Truth, whom the world cannot receive (welcome, take to its heart), because it does not see Him or know and recognize Him. But you know and recognize*

Him, for He lives with you [constantly] and will be in you."

Ephesians 1:11: *"In Him also we have obtained an inheritance, being predestined according to the purpose of HIm who works all things according to the counsel of His will."*

Acts 20:27: Paul says, *"For I have not shunned to declare to you the whole counsel of God."* You can believe that the God who called you to do it will give you the grace and the anointing with which to carry out your assignment.

Hebrews 6:17-18: *"Thus God, determining to show more abundantly to the heirs of promise the immutability of His counsel..."* What does that mean? In other words, it's impossible for God to change your assignment even if He wanted to, because He cannot change. That's what immutable means. It says, "The immutability of His counsel." What is counsel? Advice. Purpose. Assignment. Plans. God does not and cannot change. He set the parameters of His counsel in the Garden of Eden. He put His man and His woman there. He said, "The whole place is yours. Everything. Just one tree is not yours. Don't touch it. The day you eat thereof, you will surely die."

Three Kinds of Death in Scripture

There are three kinds of death in Scripture. There's spiritual death--that's what happened the day Adam and Eve ate of the forbidden fruit: it wasn't physical death. Spiritual death is the condition of your spirit. Most of the people on this earth are walking along in a body. They've toned it; they've worked it; they show it. The problem is, the man or woman inside is dead. That's the dead walking. That's spiritual death. There's physical death, and there's the second death.

Revelation 21:8 tells us, "*But the cowardly, unbelieving, abominable, murderers, sexually immoral, sorcerers, idolaters, and all liars shall have their part in the lake which burns with fire and brimstone, which is the second death.*"

That's the only death for which there's no recovery. What gets you out of that? Simply turning your life over to Jesus. His blood paid the price for you and me.

The question is, what have you done with Jesus? Are you ready to meet Him, to make Him Lord? You can pray this prayer right now. If you pray it and mean it from your heart, everything will change:

Oh, God, I realize that without Jesus, I'm lost. Without Jesus, I have no assurance of heaven. But today, I repent of my sin. I renounce it. I've turned away from it. Today, I make Jesus the Lord of my life. I say with my mouth: "Jesus, you're my Lord." I believe with my heart that God raised Jesus from the dead. Therefore, I'm saved. Praise God, I'm saved!

If you want the fire of God's counsel to burn through you, for that assignment, for that purpose, for that plan, ask God to fill you now, to let His fire fall on you today. His promises are true and He never changes.

CHAPTER 12

THE FIFTH & SIXTH FIRES: THE SPIRIT OF STRENGTH AND THE SPIRIT OF KNOWLEDGE

In this chapter, we are going to look at the next fires: the Spirit of Strength and the Spirit of Knowledge.

The Spirit of Strength:

The Hebrew word for this spirit is *gebuwrah*. It means power, it means strength, might, valor, bravery; and when used of God Himself, because God Himself moves in this, it speaks of the mighty deeds that God does.

I Chronicles 29:11-12 states *"Yours, O Lord, is the greatness, The power and the glory, The victory and the majesty; For all that is in heaven and in earth is Yours; Yours is the kingdom, O Lord, And You are exalted as head over all. Both riches and honor come from You, and You reign over all. In Your hand is power and might; In Your hand it is to make great and to give strength to all."*

Psalm 71:16 says, *"I will go in the strength of the Lord God."* We need not go anywhere, we need not say anything, unless we're going and we're speaking in the strength of the Lord God. *"I will make mention of Your righteousness, of Yours only."*

Psalm 106:2: *"Who can utter the mighty acts of the Lord? Who can declare all His praise?"*

Psalm 150:2: *"Praise Him for His mighty acts; praise Him according to His excellent greatness."*

Mark 12:30-31: "[*Jesus said,*] *'And you shall love the Lord your God with all your heart, with all your soul, with all your mind, and with all your strength.' This is the first commandment. And the second, like it, is this: 'You shall love your neighbor as yourself.' There is no other commandment greater than these.*"

2 Corinthians 1:8: Paul said, "*For we do not want you to be ignorant, brethren, of our trouble which came to us in Asia: that we were burdened beyond measure, above strength.*" Beyond measure, above our strength. That's where we are to come in, so the Spirit can supply the strength that is lacking. Paul said, "*Yes, we had the sentence of death in ourselves, that we should not trust in ourselves but in God who raises the dead, who delivered us from so great a death, and does deliver us; in whom we trust that He will still deliver us, you also helping together in prayer for us, that thanks may be given by many persons on our behalf for the gift granted to us through many.*"

1 Peter 4:11 (Darby) says, " *If any one speak — as oracles of God; if any one minister — as of strength which God supplies; that God in all things may be glorified through Jesus Christ, to whom is the glory and the might for the ages of ages. Amen.*" Ephesians 3:16 says, "*that He would grant you, according to the riches of His glory, to be strengthened with might through His Spirit in the inner man,*"

Ephesians 6:10 says, "*Finally, my brethren, be strong in the Lord and in the power of His might.*"

The Spirit of Knowledge:

The word for *knowledge* is an interesting Hebrew word: *daath.* It means discernment, perception. This is the word that is used in the Tree of Knowledge of Good and Evil. It also means skill and workmanship. This fire will provide you skill in your workmanship. It also will provide creative skill; it will provide knowledge; and it will provide knowing. Here are some Scriptures to build upon this truth:

Psalm 19:1: *"The heavens declare the glory of God."* There is no way for any human to look at the heavens and not know that God created it. *"And the firmament shows His handiwork. Day unto day utters speech."* God says the firmament—the heavens--are talking. Science is catching up with this concept. It's still so far behind God's word, but within the past several decades, scientists have proven that the sun and the other stars are speaking. The hertz levels are out of our human range, but scientists have been able to lower the hertz levels so that we can hear the voices of the stars. And they're singing! God declared this fact thousands of years ago.

That's why, when you go outside under a beautiful starlit sky, you feel closer to God, because you are hearing His voice from the heavens. *"Day unto day utters speech, and night unto night reveals knowledge."* The knowledge of God is emanating from the stars, from the heavens.

Psalm 19:3-4: *"There is no speech nor language where their voice is not heard.*

Their line is gone out through all the earth, and their words to the end of the world. In them He has set a tabernacle for the sun, which is like a bridegroom coming out of his chamber." God set up the sunrise to look like a bridegroom coming out of his chamber. That's why a sunrise is so beautiful; that's why a sunset is so beautiful. God designed it, to reveal Himself and declare His glory. *"Its rising is from one end of heaven, and its circuit to the other end; and there is nothing hid from its heat."*

Psalm 94:9-13: *"He who planted the ear, shall He not hear? He who formed the eye, shall He not see? He who instructs the nations, shall He not correct, He who teaches man knowledge? The Lord knows the thoughts of man, that they are futile. Blessed is the man whom You instruct, O Lord, and teach out of Your law, that You may give him rest from the days of adversity, until the pit is dug for the wicked."*

Psalm 139:4-9: *"For there is not a word on my tongue, but behold, O Lord, You know it altogether."* God knows what you are going to say before the thought ever gets into your head. *"You have hedged me behind and before, and laid Your hand upon me. Such knowledge is too wonderful for me; it is high, I cannot attain it. Where can I go from Your Spirit? Or where can I flee from Your presence? If I ascend into heaven, You are there; if I make my bed in hell, behold, You are there. If I take the wings of the morning, and dwell in the uttermost parts of the sea, even there Your hand shall lead me, and Your right hand shall hold me."* There are people who think they can outrun God, but they can't.

Psalm 139:10-12: *"Even there Your hand shall lead me, and Your right hand shall hold me. If I say, 'Surely the darkness shall fall on me,' even the night shall be light about me; indeed, the darkness shall not hide from You, but the night shines as the day."* God knows the point of your conception; He knows the second you were conceived:

Psalm 139:13: *"For You formed my inward parts; You covered me in my mother's womb. I will praise You, for I am fearfully and wonderfully made; marvelous are Your works, and that my soul knows very well. My frame was not hidden from You, when I was made in secret, and skillfully wrought in the lowest parts of the earth. Your eyes saw my substance, being yet unformed. And in Your book they all were written, the days fashioned for me, when as yet there were none of them. How precious also are Your thoughts to me, O God! How great is the sum of them! If I should count them, they would be more in number than the sand; when I awake, I am still with You."* Notice, the sixteenth verse of Psalm 139 says there is a book in which every detail of your assignment was recorded before you were ever born. I call this The Assignment Book. I suggest when you are praying that God's kingdom come and that His will be done right now on the earth as it is in heaven, that you ask God to download your assignment book from heaven into your spirit. Then, ask Him to bring the details of that knowledge to your understanding, so you can carry it out on a daily basis.

Ephesians 1:18: Paul said, *"The eyes of your understanding being enlightened; that you may know what is the hope of His calling, what are the riches of the glory of His inheritance in the saints."*

God's knowledge is vast, fathomless. But He is willing to share it with those who seek Him and who seek His word. His throne is the seat of His power. His kingdom authority reigns over all. And when we praise Him wholeheartedly, with abandon, He is enthroned in our praises. And that's when miracles happen.

CHAPTER 13

The Seventh Fire: the Fear of the Lord

Have you ever experienced the awe and the hush in a place, where you could hear a pin drop? That's the reverential fear of the Lord; that's the beginning of wisdom and knowledge. There are times that God is in the crescendo, but sometimes He is in the stillness. That's why we don't need to know what God is doing; we need to know God, and God will do what He's doing. Do you want to hear God? Then you're going to have to experience the fear of the Lord.

Let's look at a few scriptures, concerning this:

Psalm 99, beginning with verse 1 says, *"The Lord reigns; let the peoples tremble! He dwells between the cherubim; let the earth be moved! The Lord is great in Zion, and He is high above all the peoples. Let them praise Your great and awesome name—He is holy."*

Psalm 119:120: *"My flesh trembles for fear of You, and I am afraid of Your judgments."* There is a healthy fear of the Lord. We must have it in these days.

Jeremiah 32:38-39: *"They shall be My people, and I will be their God; then I will give them one heart and one way, that they may fear Me forever, for the good of them and their children after them."* God's purpose of giving us one heart is so that we will reverently fear Him.

We find in Luke chapter 1 that there was a priest named Zachariah, who really lacked the fear of the Lord because when the Angel of the Lord told him that he and his wife were going to have a son in their old age, he doubted. Because of that, he was struck dumb; he could not speak until the child, John the Baptist, was born.

Luke 1:63: *"And [Zacharias] asked for a writing tablet, and wrote, saying, 'His name is John.' So they all marveled. Immediately his mouth was opened and his tongue loosed, and he spoke, praising God. Then fear came on all who dwelt around them; and all these sayings were discussed throughout all the hill country of Judea."*

Then we find, in the Gospel of Luke, when Jesus worked the miracle of healing, after the paralyzed man was let down through the roof as He ministered to the people:

Luke 5:23: *"Which is easier, to say 'Your sins are forgiven you,' or to say, 'Rise up and walk?' But that you may know that the Son of Man has power on earth to forgive sins—He said to the man who was paralyzed, 'I say to you, arise, take up your bed, and go to your house.' Immediately he rose up before them, took up what he had been lying on, and departed to his own house, glorifying God. And they were all amazed, and they were filled with fear, saying 'We have seen strange things today!'"*

I noticed that there is a connection between miracles like this and the reverential fear of the Lord. Don't be surprised if this reverential fear manifests on a regular basis and suddenly miracles begin to take place: *"We have seen strange things today!"*

In Acts chapter 2:43 notice again the connection between this reverential fear and miracles. Look at this verse: *"And fear came upon every soul, and many wonders and signs were done through the apostles."* Reverential fear is awe; it shouts from the heart, "God, You're here!" What can we say?" Words are inadequate. *"And fear came upon every soul."* There is also divine judgment in this type of fear:

Acts 5, beginning with verse 1: *"But a certain man named Ananias, with Sapphira his wife, sold a possession. And he kept back part of the proceeds, his wife also being aware of it, and brought a certain part and laid it at the apostles' feet. But Peter said, 'Ananias, why has Satan filled your heart to lie to the Holy Spirit and keep back part of the price of the land for yourself? While it remained, was it not your own? And after it was sold, was it not in your own control? Why have you conceived this thing in your heart? You have not lied to men but to God.' Then Ananias, hearing these words, fell down and breathed his last. So great fear came upon all those who heard these things. And the young men arose and wrapped him up, carried him out, and buried him. Now it was about three hours later when his wife came in, not knowing what had happened. And Peter answered her, 'Tell me whether you sold the land for so much?' She said, 'Yes, for so much.' Then Peter said to her, 'How is it that you have agreed together to test the Spirit of the Lord? Look, the feet of those who have buried your husband are at the door, and they will carry you out.'"*

My friend, this was a church service! The job of the young men in that service was to bury two people. That was the youth ministry that day. *"And she fell immediately at his feet, breathed her last, and the young men came in and found her dead and carried her out and buried her beside her husband. And great fear came upon the whole church and upon all who heard of these things."*

Acts 9:31: "*Then the churches throughout all Judea, Galilee, and Samaria had peace, and were edified. And walking in the fear of the Lord and in the comfort of the Holy Spirit, they were multiplied.*"

This fear of the Lord is connected with increase. It is also connected with multiplication and with miracles.

Acts 10:34-35: "*Then Peter opened his mouth and said, 'In truth I perceive that God shows no partiality. But in every nation whoever fears Him and works righteousness is accepted by Him.'*" This illustrates having a reverential fear.

2 Corinthians 7:1: "*Therefore, having these great promises, beloved, let us cleanse ourselves from all filthiness of the flesh and spirit, perfecting holiness in the fear of God.*"

The reverential fear of God is directly related to you and me receiving the promises. God has promised healing—God says, "I want reverential fear." God has promised prosperity in your house—God says, "Give me reverential fear." God has promised direction in your life—God says, "You want direction? Give me reverential fear." You want the peace of God in your home—God says, "Give me reverential fear."

The reveential fear of God, along with the other aspects of the Seven Purifying Fires of the Holy Spirit, will help us to usher in the presence of God's throne in our lives. And where the throne of God is, the Power and Authority of the Almighty abides. May you experience this Life-Changing Power as you serve the Lord each day!

My prayer is that through a vibrant and intimate relationship with the Holy Spirit, you learn how to move into the awesome realm of tehillah praise, so that God's throne will come down in the middle of that praise. When that happens, everything the kingdom has to offer will be in your midst. You will be able to clearly hear His voice, fully embrace your assignment, and experience the kingdom itself ruling over everything you are facing in your life.

www.ingramcontent.com/pod-product-compliance
Lightning Source LLC
LaVergne TN
LVHW021358080426
835508LV00020B/2340

* 9 7 8 1 7 3 4 5 2 7 3 3 9 *